HUMANIZING THE GREATER CITY'S CHARITY

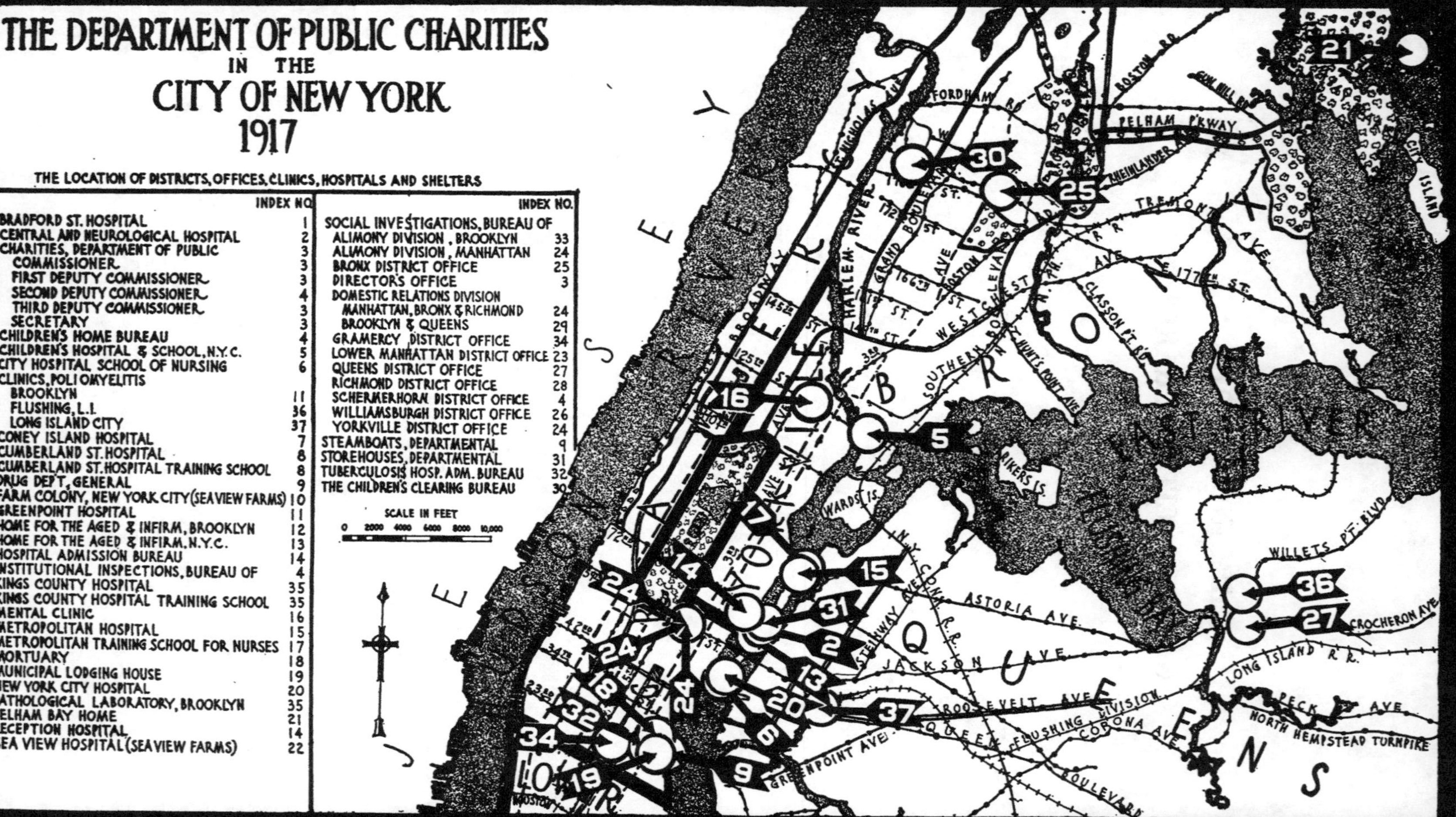

Fig. 1. Map showing the location of districts, offices and institutions of the Department of Public Charities in the City of New York, 1917.

performed by several city departments. The Department of Public Charities alone has the above offices, shelters, clinics and hospitals strategically located to meet the needs of the distressed in the greater city's five boroughs. Its investigators respond to calls from all corners of these boroughs. One institution of the department, the Pelham Bay Home, is located approximately sixteen air-line miles from the Municipal Building.

RECENT SOURCES OF INFORMATION ABOUT THE WORK OF THE DEPARTMENT OF PUBLIC CHARITIES

THE ANNUAL REPORT OF THE DEPARTMENT OF PUBLIC CHARITIES of the City of New York for 1914.

THE ANNUAL REPORT OF THE DEPARTMENT OF PUBLIC CHARITIES of the City of New York for 1915.

THE ANNUAL REPORT OF THE DEPARTMENT OF PUBLIC CHARITIES of the City of New York for 1916.

PAMPHLETS AND BULLETINS

THE CITY'S POOR IN A YEAR OF DISTRESS, *Hon. John A. Kingsbury,* a letter transmitting the 1914 Report of the Department of Public Charities to Hon. John Purroy Mitchel, Mayor.

HUMANITY AND ECONOMY IN THE CARE OF THE CITY'S POOR, *Hon. John A. Kingsbury,* a letter transmitting the 1915 Report of the Department of Public Charities to Hon. John Purroy Mitchel, Mayor.

CHILD CARING INSTITUTIONS, *Hon. William J. Doherty, Ludwig B. Bernstein, Ph.D., and R. R. Reeder, Ph.D.,* a plan of inspection, 1915.

NEW BUILDINGS, ADDITIONS AND EXTRAORDINARY REPAIRS required during 1915, 1916, and 1917.

THE MEN WE LODGE, *Robert Bertrand Brown,* a report of the Advisory Social Service Committee of the Municipal Lodging House, 1915.

EQUIPMENT, MATERIALS AND SUPPLIES used by the Department of Public Charities, 1916.

THE HOSPITAL BULLETIN, Vol. 1, No. 1, Oct. 1916; No. 2, Jan. 1917.

THE CHARITIES BULLETIN, Vol. 1, No. 1, March 1917; No. 2, April 1917; No. 3, May 1917.

HANDBOOK OF THE BUREAU OF SOCIAL INVESTIGATIONS, 1917.

BASIC QUANTITY FOOD TABLES for determining food quantities for institutional menus, July 1917.

HUMANIZING THE GREATER CITY'S CHARITY

THE WORK OF THE DEPARTMENT OF PUBLIC CHARITIES OF THE CITY OF NEW YORK

PUBLISHED BY
PUBLIC WELFARE COMMITTEE
50 EAST 42nd STREET
NEW YORK

1917

PUBLIC WELFARE COMMITTEE

Chairman
William M. Chadbourne

Vice-Chairmen
Mrs. Helen Hartley Jenkins
Adolph Lewisohn
Henry MacDonald

Treasurer
Edward P. Maynard

Chairman Finance Committee
Albert G. Milbank

Secretary
Stanley H. Howe

Henry De Forrest Baldwin
Joseph Barondess
Jacob Bashein
C. C. Burlingham
Miss Mable Choate
John Collier
Mrs. Charles Dana Gibson
Rev. Percy Stickney Grant
Mrs. William P. Earle, Jr.
William G. Hawks
Timothy Healy
Mrs. Raymond G. Ingersoll
Walter H. Liebmann
Samuel McCune Lindsay
John T. Pratt
Edward Sanderson
W. I. Scanlin
William Jay Schieffelin
Mrs. Mary Simkovitch
Wilmott Trevoy
Miss Lillian D. Wald
Mrs. Schuyler N. Warren
Mrs. Clarence Waterman

FOREWORD

THERE are three kinds of charity--the kind that comes from the heart and not from the head; the kind that comes from the head and not from the heart; and the kind that comes from the heart and the head working together.

The charity that comes from the heart and not from the head is visible everywhere. It is visible in the generous relief of so-called charitable agencies who serve no purpose of genuine charity. It is visible in the dime and quarter pressed into the outstretched hand of the chronic beggar, discouraged from honest toil by misdirected philanthropy. It blesses him that gives more than him that takes. It is like opium; it creates an appetite for more. It stimulates in the beneficiary an appetite for more charity, and in the benefactor an appetite for more smug self-satisfaction.

There is the charity which comes from the head but not from the heart. This kind of charity covers a multitude of sins. It reaches forward the right hand openly to give and backward the left hand secretly to receive. It substitutes itself for justice. It builds orphan asylums, but makes orphans. It supports widows' pensions, but makes widows. It builds playgrounds, but exploits child labor. It subserves social welfare to serve its private ends.

In the work of the Mitchel administration during the last four years, there has been a rare example of the charity that comes from the heart and the head working together. Prevention as well as relief has been the keynote of its social welfare program.

The prevention of crime has been the constant objective of the Police Department. The conviction of 1,900 fewer juvenile delinquents in 1916 than in 1913 testify that Commissioner Woods has made prevention a fact as well as a theory. Commissioner Lewis has made the Department of Correction an agency to rebuild human lives and to prevent the recurrence of delinquency.

The prevention of disease has been the faithful purpose of the Health Department. A death rate of 13.89 per thousand in 1916--the lowest ever reported in the history of the city--demonstrates that Commissioner Goldwater and Commissioner Emerson have succeeded in conserving and protecting human life.

Through its various departments, the present city administration has accomplished more for the service of the sick and the unfortunate than any city administration New York has ever had. Because the Department of Public Charities has played so important a part in that humanitarian record, the Public Welfare Committee publishes this hand-book of its work.

Because men do not like tragedy, the demands upon a public charities department are not widely known. In giving wider publicity to the work of this department, this committee wishes to call attention to some of the noteworthy features of its record. In spite of the non-exacting disinterest of a public opinion uninfluenced by the feeble voice of the 'submerged tenth'; in spite of relief demands (in 1914 and 1915) swelled by one of the most critical unemployment crises in American history; in spite of the scathing criticism of designing detractors and zealous but unenlightened citizens; in spite of political opposition which led the commissioner of public charities and his assistants through circuitous sessions of grand juries and investigating commissions; - - - in spite of such handicaps, this community has witnessed in the administration of the Department of Public Charities a rare quality of service in the public interest.

Much of the data for this book has been borrowed from various publications of the Department of Public Charities, particularly from its annual report for 1916.

The work has been organized and edited by Mr. Robert Bertrand Brown, with the aid of Miss Iulia V. Grandin and a staff of assistants. Grateful acknowledgment is here made for these services. The committee is indebted to Mr. Balfour Ker for his drawings. It has to thank those private citizens whose contributions have made possible this hand-book.

STANLEY H. HOWE,
Secretary.

CONTENTS

ILLUSTRATIONS

GRAPHS

PHOTOGRAPHS

THE PEOPLE OF THE CITY OF NEW YORK

THE MAYOR

THE COMMISSIONER OF PUBLIC CHARITIES

10TH FLOOR, MUNICIPAL BUILDING MANHATTAN

THE FIRST DEPUTY COMMISSIONER

10TH FLOOR, MUNICIPAL BLD'G. MANHATTAN

- THE GENERAL SUPERVISION OF THE INSTITUTIONAL ACTIVITIES OF THE DEPARTMENT OF PUBLIC CHARITIES, EXCLUSIVE OF THE MORTUARY AND THE MUNICIPAL LODGING HOUSE, INCLUDING THE CARE AND WELFARE OF THEIR PATIENTS AND INMATES AND THE OPERATION OF THEIR MEDICAL NURSING, DIETARY, EDUCAT'N'L, RECREATIONAL, HOUSEKEEPING AND LAUNDRY SERVICES THE ADMINISTRATION OF THE HOSPITAL ADMISSION BUREAU.
- THE GENERAL SUPERVISION OF THE REQUISITIONING, PURCHASING, MANUFACTURING, STORAGE AND DISTRIBUTION OF DEPARTMENTAL SUPPLIES AND EQUIPMENTS THE SUPERVISION OF THE DIVISION OF AUDITS AND ACCOUNTS
- THE GENERAL SUPERVISION THROUGH THE ENGINEERING DIVISION OF THE PLANNING, CONSTRUCTION AND ALTERATION OF ALL DEPARTMENTAL STRUCTURES AND BUILDINGS, REPRESENTING THE DEPARTMENT IN MATTERS WHICH REQUIRE REVIEW, CONSIDERATION OR ACTION BY THE BUREAU OF CONTRACT SUPERVISION.
- THE GENERAL SUPERVISION OF DEPARTMENTAL TRANSPORTATION AND OF THE DEPARTMENTAL STABLES AND GARAGES, EXCLUSIVE OF THE REPAIR AND UP-KEEP OF MOTOR VEHICLES AND THE OPERATION OF THE 26TH ST GARAGE

THE SECOND DEPUTY COMMISSIONER

327 SCHERMERHORN ST BROOKLYN

- THE GENERAL SUPERVISION OF THE MAJOR NON-INSTITUTIONAL RELIEF ACTIVITIES OF THE DEPARTMENT INCLUDING
  - THE BUREAU OF SOCIAL INVESTIGATIONS - FOR THE INVESTIGATION OF COMPLAINTS IN DOMESTIC RELATIONS PROCEEDINGS, AND OF APPLICANTS FOR INSTITUTIONAL RELIEF AT PUBLIC EXPENSE, INCLUDING THE COMMITMENT AND DISCHARGE OF CHILDREN FOR THE DISTRIBUTION OF RELIEF TO THE POOR ADULT BLIND AND CIVIL AND SPANISH AMERICAN WAR VETERANS, FOR THE REHABILITATION OF FAMILIES
  - THE BUREAU OF INSTITUTIONAL INSPECTIONS - FOR THE INVESTIGATION OF PRIVATE INSTITUTIONS RECEIVING MONEY FROM THE CITY AND OF THE PUBLIC INSTITUTIONS OF THE DEPARTMENT
  - THE CHILDRENS HOME BUREAU - FOR THE PLACING-OUT, BOARDING-OUT AND SUPERVISION OF DEPENDENT CHILDREN IN FOSTER HOMES
- THE SPECIAL ATTENTION TO THE CIVIC NEEDS OF THE BOROUGH OF BROOKLYN FOR THE SERVICES OF THE DEPARTMENT OF PUBLIC CHARITIES.

THE THIRD DEPUTY COMMISSIONER

10TH FLOOR, MUNICIPAL BLD'G. MANHATTAN

- THE REPRESENTATION OF THE DEPARTMENT BEFORE THE MUNICIPAL BOARDS (EXCEPT WHERE SPECIFIC ASSIGNMENTS ARE MADE TO OTHER DEPUTIES) INCLUDING REQUESTS TO THE BOARD OF ESTIMATE AND APPORTIONMENT FOR THE FIXING AND MODIFICATION OF THE DEPARTMENT BUDGET. AND ACTIONS BEFORE THE BOARD OF ALDERMAN.
- THE GENERAL CHARGE OF ALL MATTERS AFFECTING THE CIVIL SERVICE STATUS OF EMPLOYEES, INCLUDING APPOINTMENTS, REMOVALS, TRANSFERS, PROMOTIONS, DEMOTIONS, EFFICIENCY RATINGS, THE PROSECUTION OF CHARGES AND THE CONDUCTING OF HEARINGS NOT HELD BEFORE THE COMMISSIONER. THE NECESSARY ADJUSTMENT OF THE PERSONNEL TO MEET THE BUDGET REQUIREMENTS
- THE GENERAL SUPERVISION THROUGH THE SECRETARY OF THE DEPARTMENT OF THE CLERICAL AND STENOGRAPHIC FORCE OF THE CENTRAL OFFICE. THE UP-KEEP OF THE OFFICE RECORDS, FILES AND EQUIPMENT.
- THE PROMOTION OF THE EDUCATIONAL ACTIVITIES OF THE DEPARTMENT THROUGH EXHIBITS, PUBLICITY, PUBLIC MEETINGS AND PUBLICATIONS THE FURTHERANCE OF LEGISLATION AFFECTING THE DEPARTMENT AND THE IMPROVEMENT OF PUBLIC CHARITIES IN THE CITY.
- THE GENERAL SUPERVISION OF THE OPERATION OF THE MUNICIPAL LODGING HOUSE AND THE MORTUARY.
- THE SUPERVISION OF THE 26TH ST. GARAGE AND THE REPAIR AND UP-KEEP OF THE DEPARTMENT'S MOTOR VEHICLES.

JL

Fig. 2. Organization of the activities of the Department of Public Charities.

Since 1691 (when the half century old "Amsterdam in Nieu Netherlands" was seized by the English and named after the Duke of York) the City of New York has provided an executive machinery to supervise the community's charity. Since 1910 the Commissioner of Public Charities has had the power to appoint three deputies. Since 1914, each deputy commissioner has had jurisdiction over special aspects of the entire departmental problem, rather than over all activities in a geographical section of the city.

HON. JOHN PURROY MITCHEL

Mayor of the City of New York

"UNDER MAYOR MITCHEL MORE HAS BEEN DONE FOR THE ORDINARY CITIZEN OF NEW YORK THAN EVER BEFORE IN ITS MUNICIPAL HISTORY." —*Theodore Roosevelt.*

HON. JOHN A. KINGSBURY
Commissioner of Public Charities

"HE KNOWS AS MUCH ABOUT A HOME, AND WHAT GOES TO MAKE UP A GOOD HOME, AS ANY MAN IN THIS COUNTRY."

—*Lillian D. Wald.*

THE DEPARTMENT OF PUBLIC CHARITIES

of the

CITY OF NEW YORK

All mankind's concern is charity.

—Pope, *The Essay on Man.*

John A. Kingsbury	*Commissioner*
Henry C. Wright	*First Deputy Commissioner*
William J. Doherty	*Second Deputy Commissioner*
Floyd W. Fiske	*Third Deputy Commissioner*
Victor S. Dodworth	*Secretary*

1917

MR. CITIZEN, DO YOU KNOW--

That the Department of Public Charities received 2 per cent of the approximate $213,000,000 budget allowed by the City of New York in 1916? That the share of the Department of Education was 18.7 per cent; of the Police Department, 8.3 per cent; and of the Fire Department, 4.3 per cent?

That the City of New York expended through the Department of Public Charities in 1916 over $10,000,000 in serving the sick and destitute? That only four and one-half million of this amount was spent in the operation of the Department of Public Charities proper?

That during 1916, the City of New York paid over five and one-half million dollars to private charitable institutions for caring for the city's sick and destitute?

That the hospitals and homes under the jurisdiction of the Department of Public Charities provided an approximate aggregate of four and one-half million days accommodations during 1916 to the destitute sick and homeless of the city?

That there are some 3,300 employees engaged in the service of the Department of Public Charities? That there are approximately 15,000 appointments, removals, promotions, and other changes in personal service in the department annually?

That for the first time in the history of the department, all institutional buildings in which patients are accommodated, and in which foods are prepared, are completely screened?

That the Department of Public Charities, through the courtesy of the Interborough Rapid Transit Company, issues permits during the summer months to charitable organizations for free transportation of mothers and children to Bronx and Van Courtlandt Parks? That 49,548 children and their attendants received such free transportation in the summer of 1916?

MR. CITIZEN, DO YOU KNOW--

That if each person in the institutions of the Department of Public Charities should waste one slice of bread daily, the loss would amount to 1,040 loaves, valued at $52. That a year of such extravagance would mean a loss of 379,600 loaves valued at approximately $19,000? That the Department of Public Charities has introduced a rigid system to prevent this waste?

That during 1916, 25,000 pounds of pork were furnished by the piggery at the New York City Farm Colony to institutions of the Department of Public Charities?

That in order to double the helping of butter to the patients of the Department of Public Charities without an increased allowance for this purpose, economies of $35,000 would be necessary?

That the Department of Public Charities expended $7,500 to provide Thanksgiving and Christmas dinners in its institutions in 1916?

That the central bakery of the Department of Public Charities baked 3,529,363 pounds of bread during 1916? That, baked in one loaf of regulation dimensions, this bread would stretch from the City Hall, Manhattan, to Greenwich, Connecticut?

That the Bureau of Social Investigations registered approximately 140,000 needy persons seeking aid from the City of New York in 1916? That this number would populate the city of Syracuse?

That during 1916, the Bureau of Social Investigations distributed relief to 1,739 veterans of the Civil War, to 532 veterans of the Spanish-American War and to 977 blind adults?

That the Bureau of Social Investigations received during 1916 over $1,500 in part payment for the care of workmen's compensation cases in institutions of the Department of Public Charities?

MR. CITIZEN, DO YOU KNOW--

That the City of New York paid 86.5 per cent of the total maintenance costs of twenty private charitable institutions during 1916? That mere business sagacity demands that a rigid public inspection system exact specific standards of care and require honest bills for service actually rendered, from private institutions which pay but 13.5 per cent toward their own upkeep?

That the Commissioner of Public Charities established such a system when, in June 1916, he organized the Bureau of Institutional Inspections? That through this bureau, the Department of Public Charities supervises the care of over 22,000 children in the forty-eight private child-caring institutions receiving money from the city?

That in a reinvestigation by the Bureau of Social Investigations during 1916 of 21,764 normal children being supported in private institutions at public expense, over one-tenth of the number were found to be improper charges upon the city?

That the Department of Public Charities committed 3,425 children to private child-caring institutions through the Bureau of Social Investigations in 1916?

That during 1916, over 5,000 applications were made by parents, who were able to support their children at home, to the Bureau of Social Investigations of the Department of Public Charities, for the support of those children in institutions at public expense?

That for the first time in its history, the Department of Public Charities established during 1916 an agency for placing foster children in private homes. That in the last five months of 1916 this agency, the Children's Home Bureau, placed in foster homes 217 children who would otherwise have been cared for in institutions?

MR. CITIZEN, DO YOU KNOW--

That the state of Massachusetts has long been praised for the success of its child-placing system? That if its present rate of placement continues, the City of New York will place 6,000 dependent children in foster homes, in the next three years? That this record will be equivalent to that made by the entire state of Massachusetts, during that period?

That during 1916 over 13,000 family difficulties were settled in the office of the Domestic Relations Division of the Department of Public Charities? That this number exceeded by 3,000 the number referred for the action of the Domestic Relations Court?

That in 1916 approximately $600,000 in alimonies were paid to dependent members of families through the agency of the Alimony Division of the Department of Public Charities?

That for the care of the city's destitute sick, the Department of Public Charities expended over two and one-quarter million dollars during 1916? That approximately each dollar of this paid for one patient's treatment for one day in one of the department's institutions for the care of the destitute sick?

That there were 12,703 ambulance calls in the hospitals of the Department of Public Charities in 1916? That 12,453 of these were emergency calls?

That the Department of Public Charities now issues a quarterly hospital bulletin as a means of giving to the public the benefit of its wide opportunity for research and the results thereof?

That since the infantile paralysis epidemic of the summer of 1916, the Department of Public Charities has transported after-care patients to and from the city's clinics for the treatment of this disease? That this department established three clinics for the after-care of these sufferers?

MR. CITIZEN, DO YOU KNOW--

That in 1916 the City of New York, through the Department of Public Charities, paid for the confinement of 6,549 mothers in private hospitals?

That the Department of Public Charities conducts jointly with the Department of Health a Tuberculosis Hospital Admission Bureau, through which persons suffering in any stage of tuberculosis may obtain hospital, sanatoria or preventoria care?

That the Sea View Hospital of the Department of Public Charities is the finest and most complete tuberculosis hospital in the United States?

That electric lights were first installed in the wards of the Central and Neurological Hospital in December, 1916--some seventy odd years after the invention of this modern necessity?

That one of the best obstetrical wards in the country is maintained by the Department of Public Charities at the Greenpoint Hospital?

That in a police district of over 115,000 people, the new Greenpoint Hospital in Brooklyn provides the only hospital in which free care is given to children?

That the largest children's service in any hospital in the United States is maintained by the Department of Public Charities at the Metropolitan Hospital on Blackwell's Island?

That the Metropolitan Hospital on Blackwell's Island is equipped with one of the most modern kitchen buildings of any institution in this country?

That the Kings County Hospital of the Department of Public Charities is the second largest general hospital in the City of New York?

MR. CITIZEN, DO YOU KNOW--

That one of the best equipped operating rooms in any hospital in New York City is at the New York City Hospital on Blackwell's Island?

That the lowest mortality rate for infantile paralysis during the epidemic of 1916 in New York City was held at the New York City Hospital of the Department of Public Charities, where there were six deaths among eighty-five cases?

That the City of New York expended over $750,000 in 1916 to shelter destitute persons in its four institutions for the homeless? That this sum purchased over 2,000,000 daily accommodations for needy applicants to the Department of Public Charities?

That the Department of Public Charities during 1916 provided hundreds of convalescent and chronic patients, and residents of its homes with occupational work?

That at the Municipal Lodging House during 1916, permanent employment was found for 2,498 persons, and temporary employment for 1,407?

That the only dental service in any public philanthropic shelter in the United States is maintained in the newly established dental clinic at the Municipal Lodging House?

That at the Farm Colony on Staten Island, cottages are maintained by the Department of Public Charities where destitute aged couples may remain together instead of being ruthlessly torn apart and placed in separate dormitories?

That the Department of Public Charities maintains the largest almshouse in the United States--the City Home for the Aged and Infirm on Blackwell's Island? That it was this almshouse which was so severely arraigned by Charles Dickens in his "American Notes?" That the department is trying to make it in fact as well as in name a city home rather than an almshouse?

MR CITIZEN, DO YOU KNOW--

That the New York City Children's Hospital and School, maintained under the Department of Public Charities, is the largest public institution for the feebleminded in the United States?

That with an epidemic of infantile paralysis raging on Manhattan Island during the summer of 1916, not *one* case appeared at the New York City Children's Hospital and School?

That not one death resulted from the eighty surgical operations performed at the New York City Children's Hospital and School during 1916?

That until December 29, 1916, many of the boys at the New York City Children's Hospital and School had never seen a moving picture?

That the Department of Public Charities, through the New York City Children's Hospital and School, is training certain of its feebleminded patients to do domestic work? That these patients are placed in private families where they may earn money while under the supervision of the institution?

That the City of New York spent less than $15,000 during 1916 at its Mortuary for the care and preparation for burial of its dead? That this amount represented an expenditure of only a fraction over one dollar for the care of each body with which that institution was entrusted during that year?

That for the first time in the history of the Mortuary, women attendants are now at that institution to give aid and counsel to bereaved friends and relatives of the dead?

That the friends and relatives whose bereavement was lightened by the befriending service of the City Mortuary approximated 70,000 in 1916--more than the combined populations of New Rochelle, Mount Vernon and Tarrytown?

HUMANIZING THE GREATER CITY'S CHARITY

Fig. 3. Past and present homes of the administrative offices of the Department of Public Charities.

In March, 1736, as the "poor of the city were increasing and were becoming very burthensome to the inhabitants," a two-story almshouse was erected not far from the present City Hall.[1] This was called the "Public Workhouse and House of Correction." Here, the maladjusted, the sick, the homeless, the insane and the public offender were herded without discrimination. Today, the City of New York maintains under its Department of Public Charities, alone, some half a hundred institutions, bureaus and offices, equipped to minister to the distressed according to their special needs. In 1860, the executive offices of this department were established at number 1 Bond Street. In 1898, they were moved from number 66 Third Avenue to the East 26th Street Pier. Since April 1, 1914—over a century and three-quarters after the erection of the first city almshouse—the headquarters of this department have been on the tenth floor of the Municipal Building, the highest civic building in the world.

[1]The Rev. John Stanford, History of the Poor in New York City; Manual of the Corporation of the City of New York, 1862.

I. NEW YORK CITY AS PHILANTHROPIST

THE SCOPE OF THE DEPARTMENT OF PUBLIC CHARITIES

The Problem in a Nutshell

FEW citizens of New York City realize the extent of the philanthropic work which they, as members of this community, are carrying on through the agency of their Department of Public Charities. They know a great deal about their Police Department without reading a report. The effective work of that department is in evidence everywhere. The admirable and spectacular performances of the Fire Department are familiar to every school boy.

But with the Department of Public Charities the case is different. Charged though it is with the weighty responsibility of caring for the city's sick and destitute, this department often fails to receive the citizen's recognition because of the quiet and unostentatious manner in which its services are rendered.

When we think of philanthropists, we commonly think of individuals, not of communities. But the City of New York is the greatest philanthropist in the world. Through its Commissioner of Public Charities alone, it expends annually over $10,000,000 for the care of its dependents. This sum is almost double the total annual expenditure of the largest private philanthropic agency in the world -- the Rockefeller Foundation. It is almost exactly equal to the total capital of the Russell Sage Foundation. It is about one-twentieth of the annual city dollar. (Fig. 4.) Yet to meet it, the citizens of the greater city were taxed during 1916 a little less than $1.78 per capita.

If the Commissioner of Public Charities were to visit each day, Sundays and holidays included, one of the many institutions housing the city's poor, he would require some ten months to complete his tour.

The average citizen cannot appreciate the varied duties of the ununiformed forces of the Department of Public Charities—its field visitors and investigators, its desertion officers, its institu-

tional inspectors and child placing agents, its doctors and nurses, its teachers and play directors, its boat captains and crews its farmers and mechanics, and its thousands of hospital helpers, attendants and caretakers.

The average citizen does not see the visitor climbing thousands of tenement stairways to aid dependent families. He does not realize the inquiry necessary to protect his charity fund from the wiles of the impostor. He cannot witness the heart rending scenes in the hospitals. He does not see the flushed and emaciated faces of the city's sick. He does not see the 2,000,000 anxious friends annually boarding the department's boats to visit the poor on Blackwell's Island. He does not look upon that line of homeless men -- each night a regiment -- waiting expectantly at the door of the Municipal Lodging House for rations and comfortable cots. He does not see the saddened children separated from their broken-hearted mothers by illness, destitution or death, and sent among strangers. He does not know the agonies of the young unmarried mother surrendering her new-born babe or the courage of those who refuse to part from their offspring.

He does not see or hear even one of the 400 foundling babies left annually sleeping in the waiting rooms of department stores and ferry houses, crying in deserted hallways or shivering in cold ash cans. He does not shudder at the sight of one of the 15,000 destitute dead annually brought to the Mortuary for identification or burial. He does not see the stack of little coffins that go out daily to the Potter's Field. He does not hear the mother's plea for time to find means to prevent her child's body from being buried there. The average citizen does not see these things. They are not pleasant to see. Yet around them is woven the fabric of the work-a-day experiences of employees in the Department of Public Charities.

The Department's Underlying Policies

It has been the policy of the Department of Public Charities to relieve the city's needy with the utmost economy and efficiency. The department has not been blind, however, to the need for an

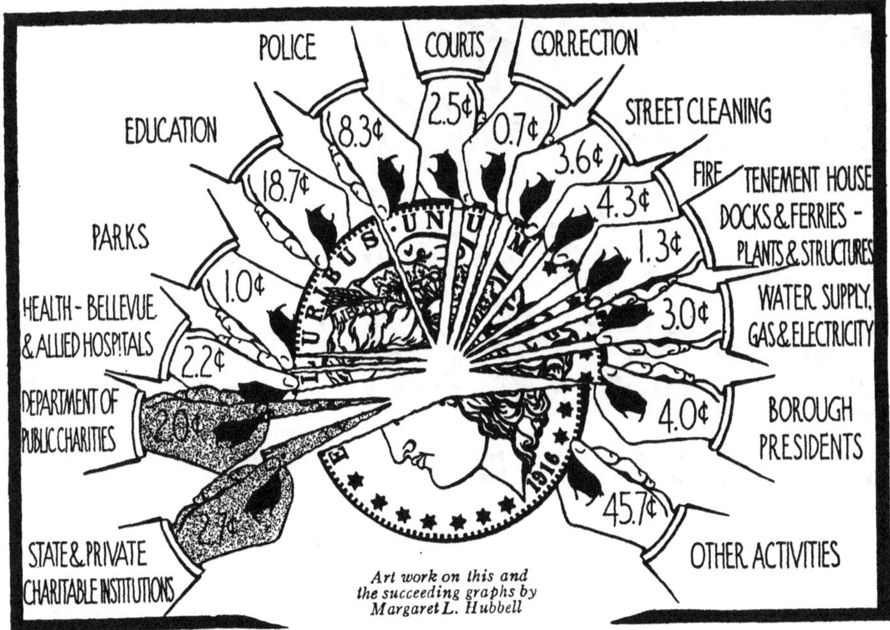

Fig. 4. Charities' share in the 1916 budget dollar of the City of New York.[2]

Approximately one-twentieth of the taxes required to meet the annual city budget go for the support of activities maintained directly and indirectly through the Department of Public Charities. Two cents out of every dollar of the 1916 budget of $212,956,177.54 went for the maintenance of activities directly under the jurisdiction of this department. Over two and one-half cents out of every dollar went for the care of city dependents approved by the commissioner of charities for care in private charitable institutions at public expense.

economy which sees the wisdom and foresight of treating the unfortunate and their ills constructively, with a view to prevention. It has seen the need for the complete segregation of the feebleminded; the maintenance of farm colonies for tramps and vagrants; the provision of hospital and colony care for inebriates and drug users; and the finding of good foster homes for normal, motherless children. The department, at the same time, has realized that wisdom, foresight and honesty must control the expenditure of the city's charities fund to the end that not one dollar of the taxpayer's money shall be either wasted or perverted. Realizing that it has no higher reason for existence than to express the sympathy of the strong for the weak, it has seen, moreover, the importance of fostering within its personnel that *esprit de corps* for humane service, lacking which its endeavors are vain.

---

[2]The Annual Report of the Department of Public Charities for the year ending December 31, 1916. Addenda, Financial Statements, B., Table 1.

Fig. 5. Recreation is a two-fold necessity to employees who come into first hand contact with the misery of the sufferers daily befriended by the Department of Public Charities.

There are some 3,300 employees required to maintain the institutions of this department. Several of these institutions are on isolated islands. The Department of Public Charities provides tennis courts, billiard rooms, libraries and club rooms for the use of many of its employees. Here is shown the library of the Kings County Hospital Training School for Nurses.

The Department of Public Charities has by no means accomplished all that it hoped to accomplish. There have been many expectations unrealized, due no doubt partly to the shortcomings of its organization and personnel, partly to not always scrupulous opposition, and partly to the unusual magnitude of the problems with which it has been called upon to cope.

HUMANIZING THE MACHINERY

OF THE DEPARTMENT OF PUBLIC CHARITIES

The Importance of a Personnel of Superior Calibre

CONSCIOUS that its physical outlay is misapplied unless manned by a personnel, competent to express the sympathy of the city which has given it origin, the Department of Public Charities, during 1916, has attempted to carry out its policy of raising the standard of character and service among its employees. (Fig. 5.) It has attempted with studied attention to keep sight of its primary reason for being -- namely, to extend sympathetic help to the thousands of dependent, destitute, defective and neglected men, women and children, who appeal to it for aid. For the performance of this task, no array of initiative, foresight, judgment, sympathy, patience, tact, intelligence, force of will power, and personal efficiency could be too great. It is a task which the machinery of the Department of Public Charities cannot meet unless manned by a personnel of superior calibre.

Improving the Quality of the Department's Personnel

In attempting to elevate the standards of its employees in the various branches of its service, the department has recently made changes in the management of some of its institutions and bureaus. Conspicuous among these have been those at the New York City Children's Hospital and School, the Cumberland Street and Coney Island Hospitals, the Children's Bureau, the Bureau of Dependent Adults, the Municipal Lodging House and the Mortuary.

As a part of its program to secure more competent and intelligent employees, the Department of Public Charities has succeeded in gradually increasing the allowances for personal service at its institutions. (Figs. 6 and 7.) In 1913, the cost of personal service in the department was $1,605,705.88. In 1916, it was $1,880,637.93. There were, in 1913, 3,098 paid employees engaged in its various activities. In 1916, there were 3,300.

The department has found that an employee who can be obtained for $5 or $10 a month is a costly servant to the city's poor.

It has attempted to eliminate the practice of employing cheap labor by the establishment of a minimum wage.

In its attempt to improve the quality of the department's personal service, monthly conferences of superintendents have been instituted. Here, problems of administration and policy are discussed. The year 1916 has marked the first codification of the general departmental instructions designed to bind the several units of the Department of Public Charities into one forceful whole.

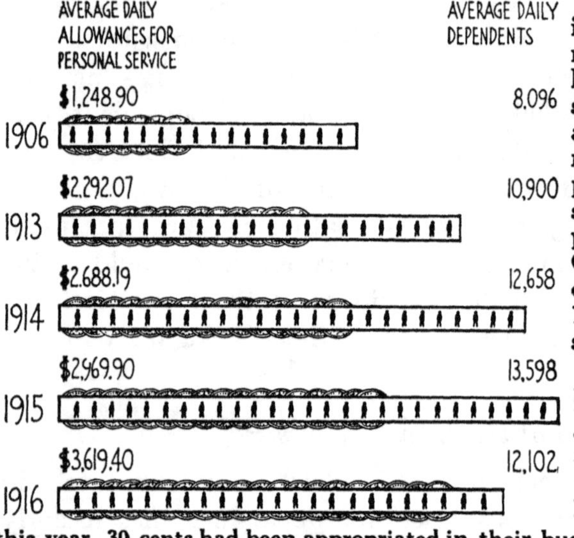

Fig. 6. Comparison between the annual average daily allowances for personal service and the annual average daily accommodations given dependents at the institutions of the Department of Public Charities, for the ending December 31, 1906, 1913–1916, inclusive.[3]

A higher amount was paid for the administration and operation of the department's institutions in 1916 than in any year heretofore. For every daily accommodation given in these institutions during this year, 30 cents had been appropriated in their budgets for personal service. That is just twice as much as had been apoprpriated for each daily accommodation they had given in 1906. The average daily number of institutional employees has increased approximately one and one-half during this decade. While the past year has witnessed a decrease of over 11 per cent in the average daily number of employees, and a similar decrease in the average daily dependents in the department's institutions, it has marked an increase of 22 per cent in the average daily allowances for personal service, and an increase of over 3 per cent in the per dependent daily allowances for such service in these institutions. The department has thus been able to give its institutional charges a higher quality of personal service than hitherto.

Comparison between the daily allowances for personal service and the daily census of dependents at the institution of the Department of Public Charities during the years ending December 31, 1906, 1913–1916, inclusive.

Source: Annual Reports of the Department of Public Charities for the respective years

Year	Average Daily Census of Institutional Dependents	Total Annual Allowances for Personal Service in Institutions	Daily Allowances for Personal Service in Institutions	Daily Allowances for Personal Service for Each Institutional Dependent
1906	8,096	$455,849.77	$1,248.90	$0.15
1913	10,900	836,605.70	2,292.07	.21
1914	12,658	981,189.01	2,688.19	.21
1915	13,598	1,084,012.08	2,969.90	.29
1916	12,102	1,324,701.04	3,619.40	.30

[3]The Annual Report of the Department of Public Charities for the year ending December 31, 1916. Addenda, Social Statistics, A., Table 1.

NEW YORK CITY AS PIONEER PHILANTHROPIST

Its Growing Civic Conscience

THE expenditure of over $10,000,000 for the care of the dependent poor through the Department of Public Charities does not mean that New York is a city of paupers. It does not mean that this city has a greater proportion of dependents than other great cities of the world, although its normal immigration does place upon it a unique and unjust burden--and one which should be borne, in the main, by the federal government. It does not mean that New York City is an unhealthy city, for its death rate compares favorably with other large cities of this country and of the world. It does not mean

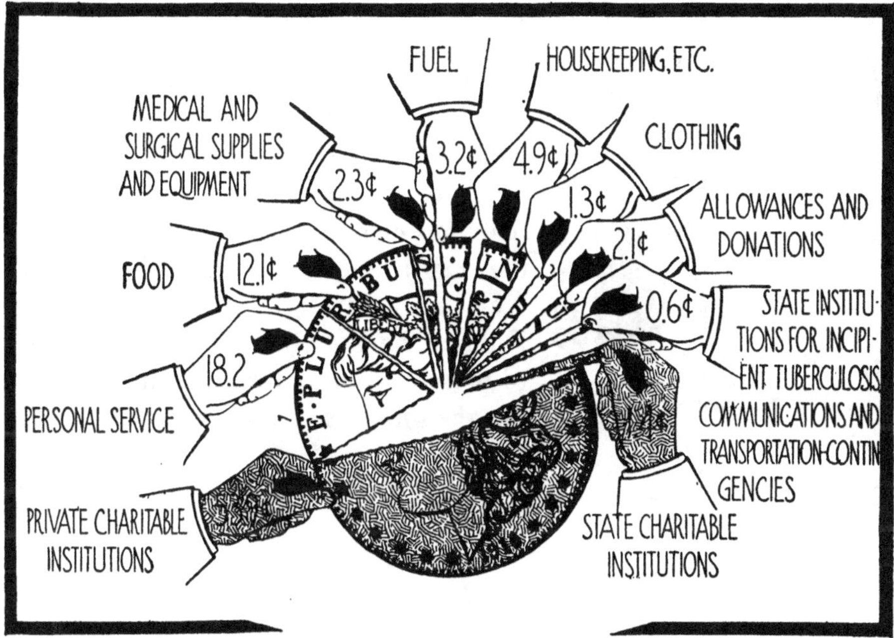

Fig. 7. The 1916 Charities dollar dissected. How it serves.[4]

Of the ten and a fraction million dollars ($10,212,971.50) spent through the agency of the Department of Public Charities for the relief of the needy of the City of New York in 1916, approximately fifty-four cents out of every dollar ($5,505,982.51) was paid to private charitable institutions for the care of city dependents. Forty-four cents out of every dollar ($4,566,792.83) was spent in maintaining the activities directly under the jurisdiction of this department. Eighteen cents of this amount went for personal service; twelve cents, for food; and approximately five cents, for general housekeeping expenses.

[4]The Annual Report of the Department of Public Charities for the year ending December 31, 1916. Addenda, Financial Statements, B., Table 5.

that it has an excessive number of feebleminded, or that insanity is more prevalent here than elsewhere. What it does mean is that the City of New York has recognized its obligations to care for the insane; to harbor and shield the feebleminded; to care for the tuberculous; to provide homes for the aged; to give shelter to the homeless and protection to orphans and abandoned children. It means, in short, that New York City some years ago began the slow and tedious process of eliminating that disgraceful institution commonly known as the almshouse, where are herded together without segregation the insane and the aged, the tuberculous and inebriate, the criminal and the dependent child. The city that boasts no poverty and prates a meagre expenditure for welfare purposes is suffering from social stagnation. It is the city which sends its tuberculous to die in a pest house; its homeless men to jail; its motherless children to asylums; and its aged to the poorhouse. With consistent reluctance to be disheartened by the magnitude of the task, the City of New York through its Department of Public Charities has continued in 1916 to pioneer with its resources in minimizing the miseries of its destitute.

II. REACHING THE NEEDY

THE WORK OF THE DEPARTMENT OF PUBLIC CHARITIES

THE Helpfulness of the Department of Public Charities must be as Versatile as the Circumstances which have Shaped the Lives of those whom it Befriends.

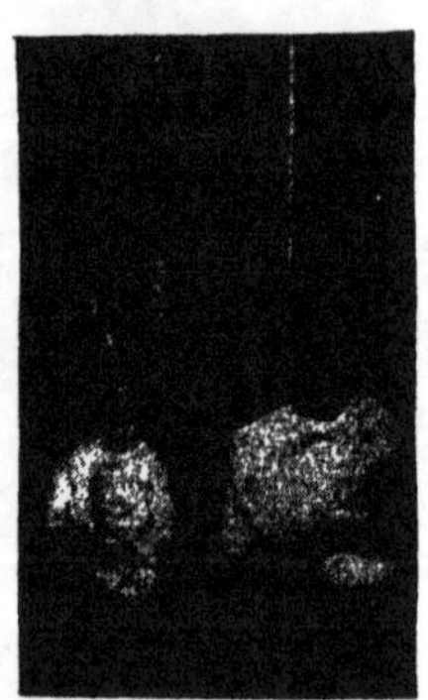

II. REACHING THE NEEDY

THE WORK OF THE DEPARTMENT OF PUBLIC CHARITIES

ADJUSTING THE MALADJUSTED

Bureaus for Inspection and Non-Institutional Relief

MISERIES are apt to be many in a city, on one block of which more than 5,000 people live on less than four acres of ground. More divers still are the personalities of the miserable. (Fig. 8.) The Department of Public Charities has organized its resources, however, to meet the needs of five general groups of dependents. (Fig. 10.) These are the maladjusted; the sick; the homeless; the feebleminded and epileptic; and the city's dead.

The major non-institutional relief activities of the department are centered in three coördinate bureaus. (Fig. 9.) These are the Bureau of Social Investigations, the Bureau of Institutional Inspections and the Children's Home Bureau. Not many citizens realize the breadth of the services offered by these bureaus. That persons fall into all manner of

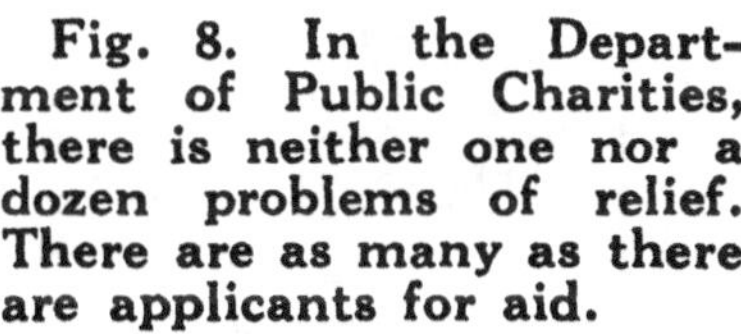

Fig. 8. In the Department of Public Charities, there is neither one nor a dozen problems of relief. There are as many as there are applicants for aid.

The helpfulness of the department must be as versatile as the circumstances which have shaped the lives of those whom it befriends. Some need help but for a night. Others require aid over a period of years. Veterans need relief; stranded strangers, transportation. Old couples need homes; dependent children, foster parents. The sick need medical care; the homeless, shelter. The subnormal need protection and training. And the bereaved need considerate counsel. But no list of generalities can express each applicant's need.

miserable circumstances, most citizens know. That such maladjustments are not adjusted mechanically, some do not know.

The Bureau of Social Investigations

Prior to 1914, the offices of the Department of Public Charities, through which the needy made application for relief, were not only inconveniently located but almost totally inco-

ADJUSTING THE MALADJUSTED

THE CHILDREN'S HOME BUREAU
327 SCHERMERHORN ST. BROOKLYN
THE PLACING OUT, BOARDING OUT AND SUPERVISION IN FOSTER HOMES OF CHILDREN BETWEEN THE AGES OF TWO AND SEVEN ACCEPTED BY THE BUREAU OF SOCIAL INVESTIGATIONS AS PUBLIC CHARGES

THE BUREAU OF SOCIAL INVESTIGATIONS
TENTH FLOOR MUNICIPAL BLD'G MANHATTAN
THE HOSPITAL DIVISION
TENTH FLOOR MUNICIPAL BLD'G MANHATTAN
THE INVESTIGATION OF PATIENTS PROPOSED BY PRIVATE HOSPITALS AS PUBLIC CHARGES AND APPLICATIONS FOR RESIDENCE IN THE HOMES FOR AGED AND INFIRM.

THE BUREAU OF INSTITUTIONAL INSPECTIONS
327 SCHERMERHORN ST. BROOKLYN
THE INSPECTION OF DEPARTMENTAL AND OF PRIVATE CHARITABLE INSTITUTIONS AND AGENCIES SUBSIDIZED BY THE CITY FOR THE CARE OF PERSONS ACCEPTED AS PUBLIC CHARGES BY THE BUREAU OF SOCIAL INVESTIGATIONS.

THE DOMESTIC RELATIONS DIVISIONS
IN MANHATTAN, BRONX AND RICHMOND
124 E. 59th ST. MANHATTAN
IN BROOKLYN & QUEENS
383 MYRTLE AVE. BROOKLYN.
THE INVESTIGATION OF COMPLAINTS IN NON-SUPPORT, ABANDONMENT, DESERTION AND BASTARDY PROCEEDINGS AND THE PRESENTATION OF SUCH MATTERS BEFORE THE PROPER COURT.

THE DISTRICT OFFICES
•IN MANHATTAN•
LOWER MANHATTAN— PEARL AND CENTER STS.
GRAMERCY— 287 FOURTH AVE.
YORKVILLE— 124 EAST 59th ST
•IN BROOKLYN•
SCHERMERHORN— 327 SCHERMERHORN ST.
WILLIAMSBURGH — 1022 GATES AVE.
•IN THE BRONX•
BRONX BERGEN B'LD'G 177th ST & TREMONT AVE
•IN QUEENS•
QUEENS TOWN HALL. FLUSHING
•IN RICHMOND•
RICHMOND BOROUGH HALL ST GEORGE
THE INVESTIGATION LEADING TO THE COMMITMENT & DISCHARGE OF NORMAL CHILDREN, TO THE ACCEPTANCE OF DEFECTIVE CHILDREN AS PUBLIC CHARGES, TO THE ADMISSION OF AGED WOMEN & COUPLES TO THE SEA-VIEW FARMS, TO THE RELIEF OF VETERANS AND POOR ADULT BLIND & TO THE REMOVAL OF ALIEN & NON-RESIDENT POOR

Fig. 9. Organization of the activities in the Department of Public Charities for adjusting the maladjusted.

In 1835, the City of New York first ordered that the commissioners of charity relieve no applicant without a proper knowledge of his claims.[5] Prior to 1915, the Bureau of Dependent Adults, the Children's Bureau and other offices operated independently in the examination of persons applying for the city's charity. These activities were reorganized in 1915 under the Bureau of Social Investigations. In 1916, the Bureau of Institutional Inspections and the Children's Home Bureau were organized.

[5]Rules for the Government of the Almshouse of the City of New York, p. 11. 1835.

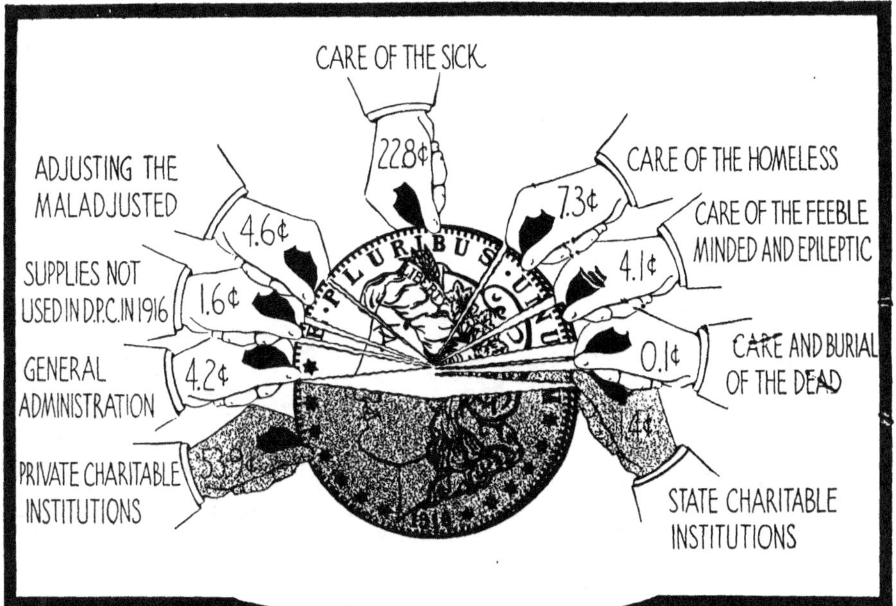

Fig. 10. The 1916 Charities dollar dissected. Whom it serves.[6]

A little over half (22.8c out of each 44.7c) of the entire amount expended in 1916 for activities directly under the jurisdiction of the Department of Public Charities went for the care of the sick in the department's eleven hospitals and thirty odd clinics. About one-sixth of the entire amount was spent in maintaining the four shelters for the homeless. Less than one-tenth was spent on general departmental administration.

ördinated. Poor persons living in the Bronx were compelled to journey to Manhattan to apply for aid. No special attention was given to the needs of the families of applicants. Investigators from one bureau would climb the same stairways in the same tenements as investigators from other bureaus, asking the same questions of the same people, but for different purposes. Duplication of effort and ineffective relief were the result.

In the early months of 1915, the bureaus for dependent adults and children were consolidated in the Bureau of Social Investigations. Offices of this bureau were placed in localities available to the residents of each of the city's boroughs. Problems of dependency are now considered from the standpoint of the family unit rather than the individual unit. But one investigator represents the department in the rehabilitation of a dependent family. Cooperation is maintained with other relief giving agencies.

---

[6]The Annual Report of the Department of Public Charities for the year ending December 31, 1916. Addenda, Financial Statements, B., Table 4.

During 1916, the Bureau of Social Investigations made 139,939 investigations. (Fig. 11.) Over 40 per cent of these were made by its Hospital Division. (Fig. 12.) This division was established in 1916 to pass upon the eligibility of patients of

Fig. 11. Action taken by the Bureau of Social Investigations on 111,165 applications for care at public expense during the year ending December 31, 1916.[7]

There were 139,939 applications for relief investigated by the 104 social investigators of the Bureau of Social Investigations during 1916. Of this number, 61,101 were made to the hospital division, and 50,064 to the district offices. The information gathered by these investigators resulted in the approval of over 70 per cent (or 78,234), and in the disapproval of the remaining 30 per cent (or 32,931) of these applications. Among those approved were applicants for institutional care at public expense, veterans and blind persons seeking pensions, and strangers to be returned to their places of legal residence. Among those disapproved were persons able to support themselves, residents of other cities and states, and persons who for other reasons were considered improper public charges.

private hospitals and residents of the city homes to receive care at the city's expense.

Seventeen per cent of the bureau's investigations were made by the Division of Domestic Relations. This division investigates complaints made by deserted parents, wives and unmarried mothers in non-support, abandonment, desertion and bastardy proceedings, adjusting such complaints or presenting its findings to the courts. (Fig. 13.) For persons whom it had befriended this unit collected (through its Alimony Bureau) $598,755 from delinquent relatives in 1916. (Fig. 14.)

Thirty-eight per cent of the applications for relief, received by the Bureau of Social Investigations during 1916, came through its district offices. (Fig. 15.) There are eight of these

[7]The Annual Report of the Department of Public Charities for the year ending December 31, 1916. Addenda, Social Statistics, B., Tables 1, 2, 3 and 5.

throughout the city. They make investigations leading to the commitment and discharge of destitute, defective and neglected children as public charges, to the admission of the aged to the city's homes, to the relief of veterans and the poor adult blind, and to the transportation and deportation of non-resident and

Fig. 12. Action taken by the Hospital Division of the Bureau of Social Investigations on 61,101 cases, submitted by private hospitals for public support, during the year ending December 31, 1916.[8]

The Hospital Division of the Bureau of Social Investigations was first organized for intensive service early in 1916. A physician was made head of the division's staff. This department of the bureau investigates cases proposed by private hospitals for public support. The division's approval or disapproval is largely influenced by the extremity of the patient's need for hospital treatment and by his financial ability to pay for it. In 1916, for the first time, the Department of Public Charities agreed to pay for pre-natal treatment in private hospitals. There were during 1916, 61,929 applications for care in private hospitals at public expense. Of the 61,101 of these upon which the Hospital Division acted, 33,921 (or 72 per cent) were approved. These applications were made in behalf of 17,131 applicants who had received surgical treatment; 13,532, who had received general medical treatment; 6,205 children under five years of age; 5,494 maternity patients and others.

alien dependents. The number of children approved for commitment to private charitable institutions at public expense, dropped to 3,630 during 1916. (Fig. 16.) Much of this reduction resulted from a more intensive and careful consideration of each applicant by the bureau. (Figs. 17 and 18.) During the year, the district offices of the Bureau of Social Investigations investigated 21,764 children, who had been previously committed to institutions. (Fig. 19.) As a result, over 12 per cent of them

[8]The Annual Report of the Department of Public Charities for the year ending December 31, 1916. Addenda, Social Statistics B. Table 2.

Fig. 13. Office settlements in the 24,184 cases counseled and aided by the Domestic Relations Division of the Bureau of Social Investigations during the year ending December 31, 1916.[9]

Aged and dependent parents turn to this division for support from their children. Unmarried and deserted mothers are referred here for aid in their domestic difficulties. Of the 24,184 cases brought before the Domestic Relations Division during the year, 74 per cent (or 17,906) involved abandonment of children by parents or of wives by husbands; 20 per cent (or 4,844) involved non-support by the legally responsible breadwinner; and the remaining 6 per cent (or 1,434) involved actions by unmarried mothers against the fathers of their children. Over 55 per cent (or 13,374) of all of these were settled in the office of the division without recourse to the Domestic Relations Courts. The number of arraignments in the Children's Courts and the Women's Night Court are also decreased, no doubt, through the influence of this division.

were removed. (Fig. 20.) In 1916, the City of New York placed at the disposal of these offices $151,000 for the relief of veterans of the Civil and Spanish-American Wars. (Fig. 21.)

The Bureau of Institutional Inspections

The Charter of the City of New York requires the Commis-

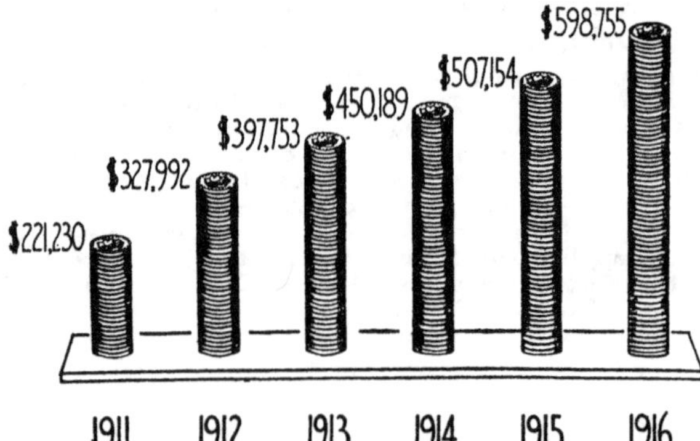

Fig. 14. Increase in the moneys received by the Alimony Division of the Division of Domestic Relations, for payment to dependent members of families during the years ending December 31, 1911-1916, inclusive.[10]

Through the Bureau of Social Investigations, the Department of Public Charities co-operates with the Domestic Relations Courts in collecting from delinquent relatives support for persons who otherwise would be apt to become public charges. Aged parents, deserted and unmarried mothers are aided in this way. In the last six years, over two million dollars ($2,503,072.46) have been collected by the Department of Public Charities for these persons. In his 1914 report to the mayor, the commissioner of charities pointed out that 20 per cent of the children supported in institutions at the city's expense "were made destitute as a result of wilful desertion by the parent."[11] The establishment of a Desertion Bureau in 1916 marked the beginning of a system whereby men who wilfully abandon their wives and children may be apprehended and brought to justice.

---

[9] The Annual Report of the Department of Public Charities for the year ending December 31, 1916. Addenda, Social Statistics B, Table 4.

[10] The Annual Report of the Department of Public Charities for the year ending December 31, 1916. Addenda, Financial Statements, D., Table 4.

[11] The 1914 Annual Report of the Department of Public Charities, p. 45.

sioner of Public Charities, as Overseer of the Poor, to approve all bills submitted to the city by private charitable institutions for the shelter and care of public charges. (Fig. 23.) The formation of a bureau of institutional inspections became impera-

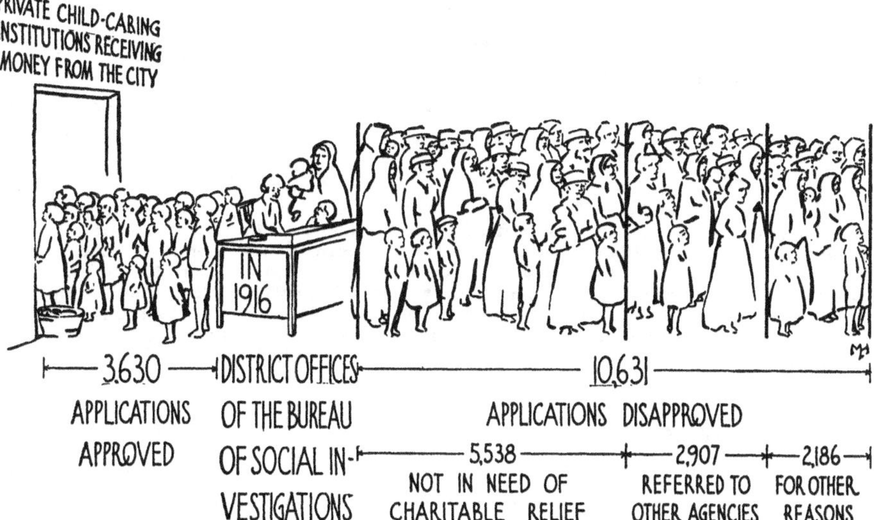

Fig. 15. Action taken by the district offices of the Bureau of Social Investigations on the 14,261 applications for the commitment of normal children to institutions during the year ending December 31, 1916.[12]

Through the Department of Public Charities, the City of New York places dependent children under sixteen years of age in private charitable institutions for care and training. Applications for such care are made to the district offices of the Bureau of Social Investigations. During 1916, 14,585 such applications were made. The offices passed upon 14,261 of these during the year, approving 3,630 (or 25 per cent) of them Of the 10,631 applications disapproved, 5,538 (or 52 per cent) were adjudged not to be in need of relief (5,110 being considered able to be supported in their own homes), and 2,907 (or 27 per cent) were referred to other agencies such as the Board of Child Welfare, the Children's Courts and the private relief societies. Other reasons for disapproval were the withdrawal of applications on the part of applicants, non-residence in the city, and the giving of false and insufficient information.

tive in 1916, when the State Board of Charities ceased to report to the Commissioner of Public Charities on the conditions existing in these private institutions receiving money from the City of New York. This action by the State Board of Charities was precipitated by the Strong inquiry, which was initiated by Governor Whitman following the investigation of an advisory committee secured by the commissioner of charities to inquire into the conduct of affairs in these institutions. Although the city

[12]The Annual Report of the Department of Public Charities for the year ending December 31, 1916. Addenda, Social Statistics, B., Tables 5 and 8.

had for some years paid the bulk of the maintenance cost of some of these institutions (Fig. 24), it had previously had little information regarding their management.*

Fig. 16. Decrease in the number of New York City Children approved for commitment to private charitable institutions through the Bureau of Social Investigations, during the years ending 1907-1916, inclusive.[14]

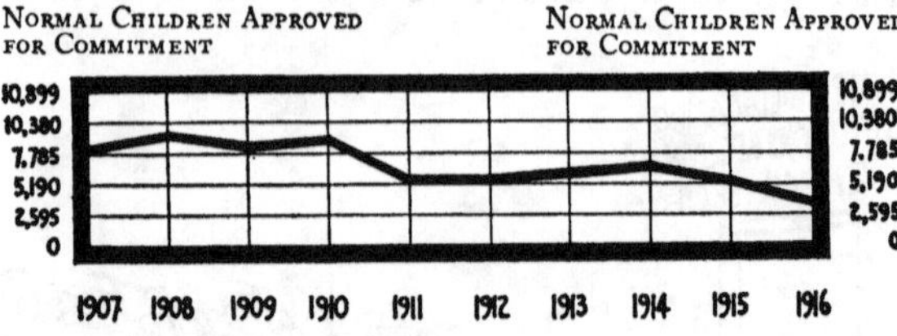

This curve shows the effect of recent concentration by the Department of Public Charities upon the problem of the dependent child. In 1908, the department approved over 9,500 applications for the commitment of normal children to private charitable institutions. For the first time in over ten years, the number of such approvals dropped to less than 3,700 in 1916. Increased co-operation by private relief societies; recent legislative provisions for the pensioning of widows and for the compensation of injured workmen: and the general improvement of industrial conditions are factors which have aided in effecting this decrease.

Legally and morally responsible for the care and well-being of their charges, among whom were over 22,000 dependent and delinquent children (Fig. 24), the charities commissioner was not content to approve perfunctorily bills sent him by private hospi-

[13]In 1911, the Comptroller and the present Mayor as a special committee of the Board of Estimate and Apportionment, undertook to inform themselves concerning the conditions surrounding the city's 22,000 orphaned and dependent children, who, for the most part, are normal in mind and body, and are cared for in private institutions largely at public expense. Referring to this investigation, the Comptroller said: "There are few departments of municipal activity concerning which there is so little information available to the public as those regarding activities which relate to the care of dependent children. . . . This condition of aloofness, with respect to the management of private institutions, has been characteristic of even the Department of Public Charities, which is the medium through which the great majority of the dependent children now maintained in private charitable institutions at the city's expense have been committed." This was the initial forward step taken by the city government to secure a more satisfactory accounting for the $5,500,000 annually appropriated to pay for public charges committed to these institutions by the Commissioner of Public Charities. Without the cooperation of the Department of Public Charities, the arm of the government responsible for the welfare of these children, the efforts of this special committee of the Board of Estimate and Apportionment were necessarily restricted.

*APPLICATION APPROVED BY THE BUREAU OF SOCIAL INVESTIGATIONS FOR THE COMMITMENT OF NORMAL CHILDREN TO INSTITUTION, DURING THE YEARS ENDING DECEMBER 31, 1907—1916.

Year	Applications approved for commitment	Sources Reference to annual reports of the Department of Public Charities for the respective years
1907	8,381	Pages 329–551–579
1908	9,549	Pages 381–639–668
1909	8,672	Pages 26–71–80
1910	9,130	Pages 28–70–79
1911	5,804	Pages 52–142–176
1912	5,767	Pages 45–164–192
1913	6,200	Pages 65–222–257
1914	6,799	Pages 120–148–170
1915	5,520	The Bureau of Social Investigations
1916	3,630	Addenda, Social Statistics, Table B-5

tals, homes for aged and incurables, and by children's institutions without any knowledge of the honesty of these bills or of the service actually rendered by these institutions. Deprived of an adequate reporting agency, he consulted with the Mayor, the Comptroller and the Corporation Counsel and, upon their ad-

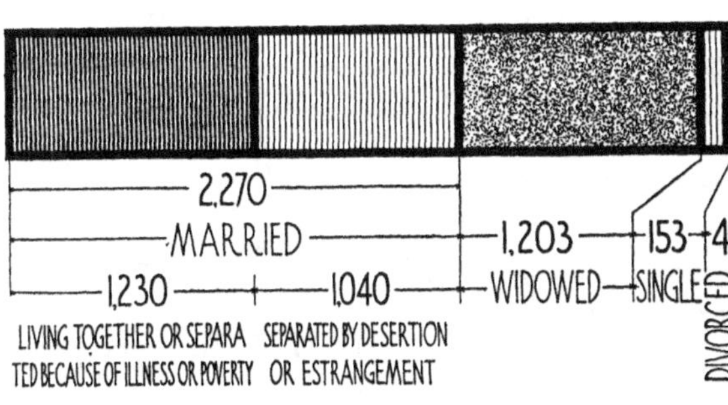

Fig. 17. Marital condition of the parents of the 3,630 children approved for commitment to private child-caring institutions by the district offices of the Bureau of Social Investigations during the year ending December 31, 1916.[15]

In sixty-two cases out of a hundred, the parents of the children approved for commitment were married. In twenty-eight of these cases they were separated by desertion or estrangement. (The Department of Public Charities organized a desertion bureau in 1916 as a part of a plan to apprehend those who attempt thus to avoid the responsibilities of parenthood.) In thirty-three cases out of every hundred, the parents of children approved for commitment were widowed. That only 153 of the parents were single is partial evidence of the value of the work of the Division of Domestic Relations in obtaining support for unmarried mothers.

vice, made application before the Board of Estimate and Apportionment and the Board of Aldermen for a force of inspectors to report regularly upon the conditions existing in every charitable institution and agency receiving money from the City of New York. The establishment of the Bureau of Institutional Inspections resulted.

Initial reports of this new bureau show that a number of these institutions have improved materially. Dormitory, bathing and toilet facilities have been modernized. The medical service in some of the institutions has been extended, and most of them now have salaried dentists. Individual chairs have replaced backless benches in the dining rooms, and children are no longer required to remain silent during the meal hour. Institutional uniforms have given place

15The Annual Report of the Department of Public Charities for the year ending December 31, 1916. Addenda, Social Statistics B, Table 7.

to clothing varied in pattern and design. Modern methods of instruction have been introduced into the school rooms. Vocational training no longer means the accomplishment of the institution's routine work by the exploitation of dependents. It means training in carpentry, cookery, dressmaking, sewing, millinery, stenography and typewriting. Increased attention is being given to the social and recreational life of institutional charges. Reports of this bureau show that these wards were given a squarer deal in 1916 than at any time heretofore.

The Children's Home Bureau

The White House

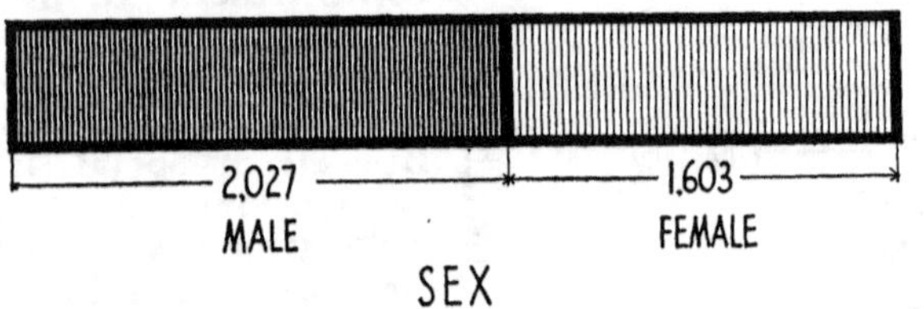

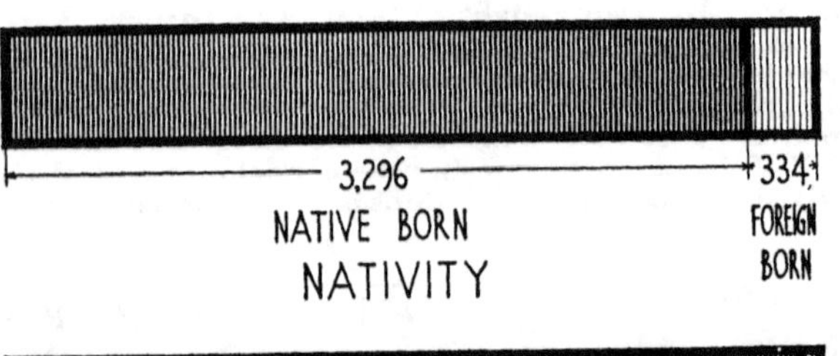

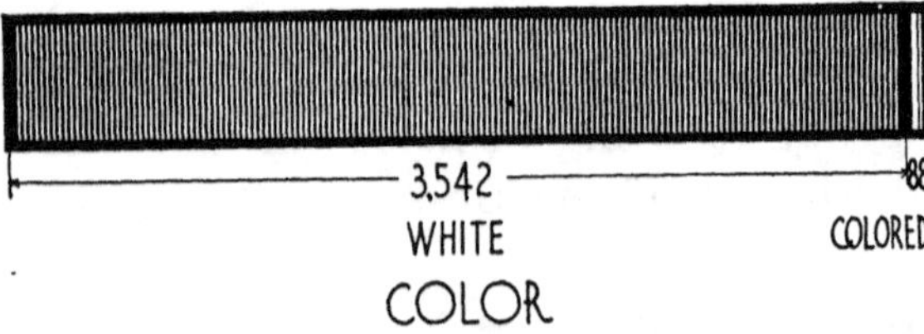

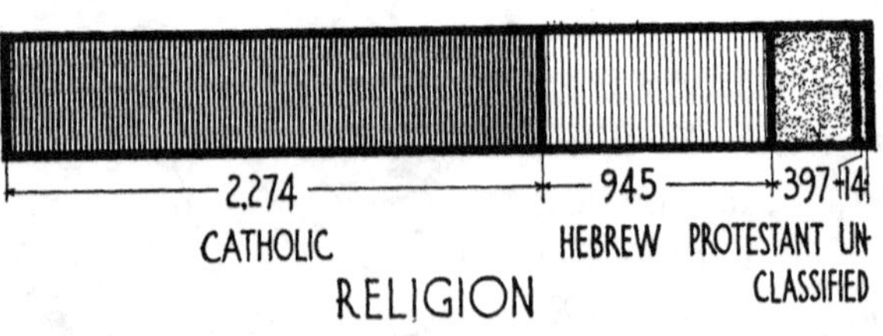

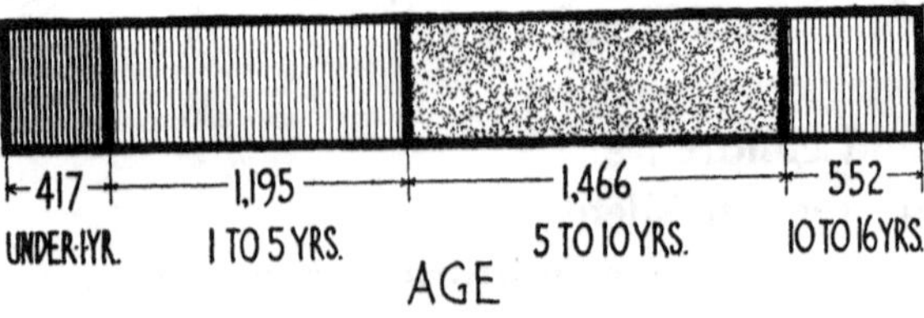

Fig. 18. Composition and characteristics of the 3,630 children approved for commitment at public expense to private charitable institutions by the district offices of the Bureau of Social Investigations during the year ending December 31, 1916.[16]

The City of New York is a foster parent unprejudiced by race, color or religion. Among the 3,630 children approved in 1916 by the Department of Public Charities for support in private institutions, were representatives, from the various component elements of the city's population. As might be expected, 91 per cent (or 3,296) of them were native born. The remaining 9 per cent (or 334) were natives of two dozen or more foreign countries, 56 per cent (or 2,027) of them were males, 44 per cent (or 1,612) of them were under five years of age.

16The Annual Report of the Department of Public Charities for the year ending December 31, 1916. Addenda, Social Statistics, B., Table 6.

Fig. 19. Children committed at public expense to private charitable institutions through the Department of Public Charities and through other sources during the year ending December 31, 1916.[17]

During 1916, 8,641 children under sixteen years of age were supported in private institutions at the expense of the City of New York. About 40 per cent of these had been committed through the Department of Public Charities because of the illness, poverty or death of their legally responsible bread-winner. Thirty-four per cent had been committed through the Children's Courts on account of their delinquency or because of the immorality or neglect of their parents. Approximately 12 per cent were surrendered directly to the institutions by their parents.

public sentiment on record as against the institutional rearing of dependent normal children. Expressing the spirit of that conference before the Sixtieth Congress of the United States President Roosevelt said: "Home life is the highest and finest product of civilization. Children should not be deprived of it except for urgent and compelling reasons." For some time, the

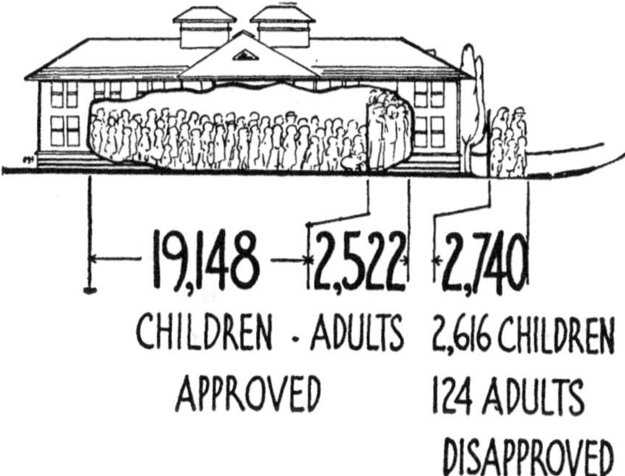

Fig. 20. Decisions rendered by the Bureau of Social Investigations (during the year ending December 31, 1916) in 24,410 reinvestigations to determine the eligibility of institutional charges for care at public expense[12].

Through the gratuity of the City of New York, an aggregate of over twelve million days of shelter and care was given the needy through the Department of Public Charities in 1916. In a reinvestigation of 24,410 of the persons receiving these accommodations, the Bureau of Social Investigations found that 2,740 of them were not dependent upon public charity for support. Every eighth one of the 21,764 public charges investigated in the private child-caring institutions had some relative who was able to support him. Four out of every hundred of the 2,646 persons investigated in the homes of the Department of Public Charities did not require the city's charity. By their removal, the department will have saved over $13,000 within a year on the maintenance cost of its homes.

---

[17]The Annual Report of the Department of Public Charities for the year ending December 31, 1916. Addenda, Social Statistics, C., Table 2.

[18]The Commissioner or Deputy Commissioner shall have power to commit; to indenture, *place out,* discharge or transfer any child who may be in his custody . . . . whenever, in his judgment, it shall be for the best interests of the child so to do." . . . . Charter of the City of New York, Sec. 664.

Department of Public Charities has seriously considered availing itself of the power vested in the commissioner of charities to place dependent children in private boarding homes,[18] but action was deferred until there was full assurance that the change in system could be operated successfully in the interests of the children.

Fig. 21. Increase in the total public relief given to veterans of the Spanish-American War and their families through the Bureau of Social Investigations, 1912-1916, inclusive.

The charter of the City of New York permits the Commissioner of Charities to give outdoor relief only to the adult blind and to war veterans and their families. During the past five years, there has been a steady increase in the relief given to veterans of the Spanish-American War. Recent increases have been, in part, due to the higher cost of living and, in part, to the registration of widows of veterans among the department's beneficiaries. The Board of Child Welfare does not grant pensions to widows who are eligible to this relief.

1912	1913	1914	1915	1916
$3,600.00	$5,295.00	$15,188.00	$28,212.00	$46,332.50

The recent Strong inquiry revived the public's interest in the home care of destitute children. The Department of Public Charities crystallized this sentiment into a tangible plan for finding homes for its wards. Private funds were secured for the operation of a placing-out bureau for an experimental period. This new activity was established in June, 1916, as the Children's Home Bureau. Before the end of the year, a clinic had been established for the examination of children before placement, and a temporary shelter had been provided for them. (Figs. 26, 27 and 28.)

As soon as public announcement was made of the organization of the bureau, some 1,500 applications for children were received. Each application was thoroughly investigated. These investigations resulted in the elimination of three-fourths of the applicants. By the end of 1916, 217 children had been placed in private homes. (Fig. 29.) Invariably children were placed with families of their own religious faith.

Balfour Ker

THE CARE OF THE SICK

The City's Fortifications Against Disease

IN 1848, the City of New York established the first public institution solely for the care of the sick. (Fig. 30.) To-day, it maintains eleven hospitals under the Department of Public Charities alone. (Fig. 22.) Through these institutions, this department brought relief to over 6,000 patients daily, in 1916.

The nature of the service given in these hospitals is three-fold. General care is given the sick at the New York City and Metropolitan Hospitals on Blackwell's Island (Figs. 31 and 32); and at the Kings County, Cumberland Street, Coney Island, Greenpoint and Bradford Street Hospitals in Brooklyn. (Figs. 33 to 37.) Special care is given to tuberculous patients at the Sea View Farms (formerly the Sea View Hospital) on Staten Island, and to patients with nervous diseases at the Central and Neurological Hospital on Blackwell's Island. Care is given to convalescent mothers and babies at the Pelham Bay Home on Hunter's Island. (Fig. 38.) The medical service at most of these institutions is supplemented by social after-care.

The General Hospitals

There are seven general hospitals under the supervision of the Department of Public Charities. More prompt and efficient service to the city's sick resulted in 1916 from the inauguration of a new reporting system in these hospitals informing the commissioner of charities of the diagnosis of each patient upon admission, the working diagnosis of the attendant treating him and the final diagnosis of his case. (Figs. 39 to 41.)

The law providing compensation for injured workmen placed additional responsibilities on the hospitals other than the mere treatment of the afflictions with which these workmen suffered. A plan for reporting these cases was found necessary in order to establish a basis of charge. Per diem fees for treatment were fixed. A procedure was established for notifying employ-

THE CARE OF THE DESTITUTE SICK

THE CONVALESCENT CARE

THE PELHAM BAY HOME
PELHAM BAY, N.Y.
THE CARE OF CONVALESCENT WOMEN, INCLUDING MOTHERS WITH BABIES ONE YEAR OF AGE AND UNDER. THE INSTRUCTION OF MOTHERS IN CHILD CARE.

THE GENERAL CARE

THE RECEPTION HOSPITAL
FT. OF E. 70TH ST. MANHATTAN
THE ADMISSION OF PATIENTS TO THE CITY, METROPOLITAN AND CENTRAL AND NEUROLOGICAL HOSPITALS ON BLACKWELLS ISLAND (MANAGED JOINTLY WITH THE METROPOLITAN HOSPITAL)

THE METROPOLITAN HOSPITAL
BLACKWELLS ISLAND
THE TREATMENT OF GENERAL ILLNESS INCLUDING TUBERCULOSIS AND CHILDRENS DISEASES

THE SPECIAL CARE

THE CENTRAL & NEUROLOGICAL HOSPITAL
BLACKWELLS ISLAND
FOR THE TREATMENT OF NERVOUS DISEASES (MANAGED JOINTLY WITH NEW YORK CITY HOSPITAL)

THE SEA VIEW FARMS
(FORMERLY THE SEAVIEW HOSPITAL)
CASTLETON CORNERS STATEN ISLAND
THE TREATMENT OF ALL STAGES OF TUBERCULOSIS

THE NEW YORK CITY HOSPITAL
BLACKWELLS ISLAND
THE TREATMENT OF GENERAL ILLNESS

THE GREENPOINT HOSPITAL
KINGSLAND AVE & JACKSON ST, BROOKLYN.
THE TREATMENT OF GENERAL ILLNESS

THE BRADFORD STREET HOSPITAL
113 BRADFORD STREET BROOKLYN
THE EMERGENCY & DISPENSARY TREATMENT OF GENERAL ILLNESS (MANAGED JOINTLY WITH THE KINGS COUNTY HOSPITAL)

THE CUMBERLAND STREET HOSPITAL
109 CUMBERLAND STREET BROOKLYN
THE TREATMENT OF GENERAL ILLNESS

THE KINGS COUNTY HOSPITAL
CLARKSON ST. & ALBANY AVE BROOKLYN
THE TREATMENT OF GENERAL ILLNESS

THE CONEY ISLAND HOSPITAL
OCEAN PARKWAY & AVE. Z. BROOKLYN.
THE TREATMENT OF GENERAL ILLNESS

JL

Fig. 22. Organization of the activities in the Department of Public Charities for the care of the sick.

The department's ten hospitals and one convalescent home provide an aggregate of over 6,000 beds for the care and treatment of general illness. These institutions operate some thirty odd clinics. Seven of them have departments for the social after-care of their patients. The newest hospital under the Department of Public Charities is the Greenpoint Hospital, opened in 1915. In 1916, an appropriation of $600,000 was allowed for the erection of a new Cumberland Street Hospital.[19]

ers of the nature of employees' injuries and for transmitting this information to the New York State Industrial Commission.

During the summer, the Hospital Admission Bureau of the department was removed from the East Twenty-sixth Street pier to the Reception Hospital at the foot of East Seventieth Street. This location makes the bureau more accessible to the hospitals

[19] Fig. 116, p. 130.

on Blackwell's Island. It was brought with the Reception Hospital (Fig. 43) under the control and supervision of the superintendent of Metropolitan Hospital. Policies were formulated regarding the types of patients to be transferred to the various departmental hospitals. This differentiation in the disposition and treatment of the sick improved the quality of the hospital service materially. Homeless applicants for admission to the city's permanent shelters formerly admitted through this bureau are now received at the Municipal Lodging House. Here, they may receive temporary accommodations pending their transfer to the city's homes.

An addition to the Greenpoint Hospital was opened in June, 1916. An appropriation of $600,000 was allowed on December 27, 1916, for a new building to house the activities of the Cumberland Street Hospital. New forms of medical organization and supervision have been put into effect at both of these hospitals. Following the plan of administration of the Johns Hopkins and the Massachusetts General Hospitals, they divide their functions into four branches of service, namely: medical, surgical, gynæcological and obstetrical. (Fig. 42.) The out-patient work of these two institutions

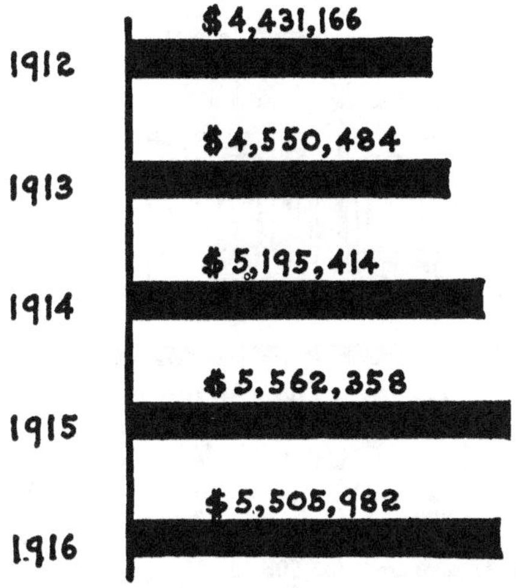

Fig. 23. Yearly expenditures by the City of New York for the care of dependents and delinquents committed to private charitable institutions, 1912-1916, inclusive.[20]

The City of New York pays for the care in private charitable institutions of dependents and delinquents admitted through the courts and through the Department of Public Charities. The gradual increase of public expenditures for this purpose may be partially accounted for by the recent unemployment crisis, which effected the relief curve of the Department of Public Charities at every point. The industrial situation had not improved sufficiently to permit the removal of many public charges from institutions in 1915. The city paid $56,376 less in 1916 than in 1915 for such charges. This is no doubt due in part to the improved economic conditions. The more intensive investigation of applications for institutional relief made by the Bureau of Social Investigations (organized in 1915) is perhaps another factor which helped to effect this decrease.

[20]The Annual Report of the Department of Public Charities for the year ending December 31, 1916. Addenda, Financial Statements, B. Table 1. The expenditures in 1914 and in 1916 exceeded the original budgetary allowances by $153.95 and $221,107.51 in the respective years. See Table 2.

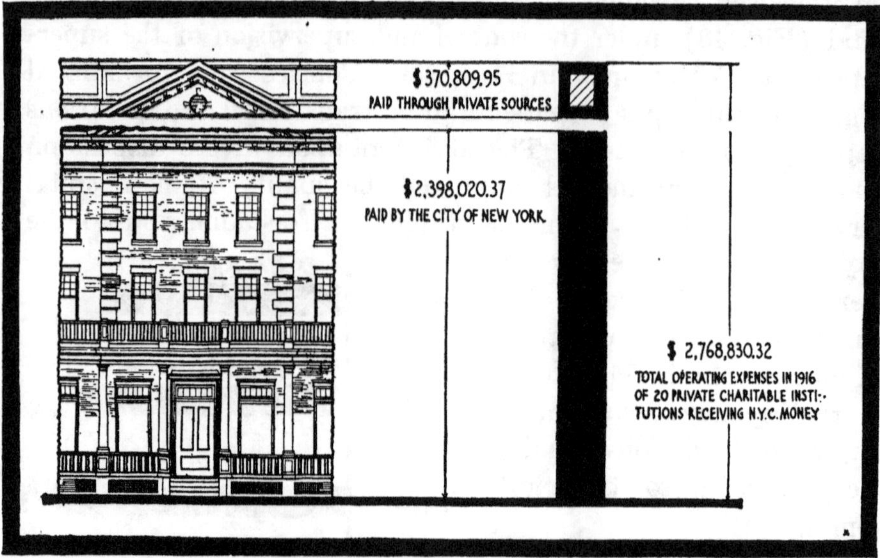

Fig. 24. Over 86 per cent of the total operation costs of twenty private charitable institutions were paid out of the 1916 charities fund of the City of New York.[21]

The total amount paid by the city to these twenty institutions in 1916 was $2,398,020.37. This was 23 per cent of the total funds ($10,212,917.50) expended through the Department of Public Charities. It made up over 43 per cent of the total amount ($5,505,082.51) paid by the city to private charitable institutions during the year. Because business sagacity demands that the substantial contributors to an enterprise know something of the way in which that enterprise is being managed, the commissioner of charities (who is the agent of the city in the expenditure of its charities funds) has recently established the Bureau of Institutional Inspections as an effective organization for reporting on the conditions existing in all charitable institutions receiving city money.

during the year has merited especial attention. A pre-natal clinic has been established at the Cumberland Street Hospital to provide treatment and instruction to mothers anticipating confinement. During the first year of its maintenance, the clinic per-

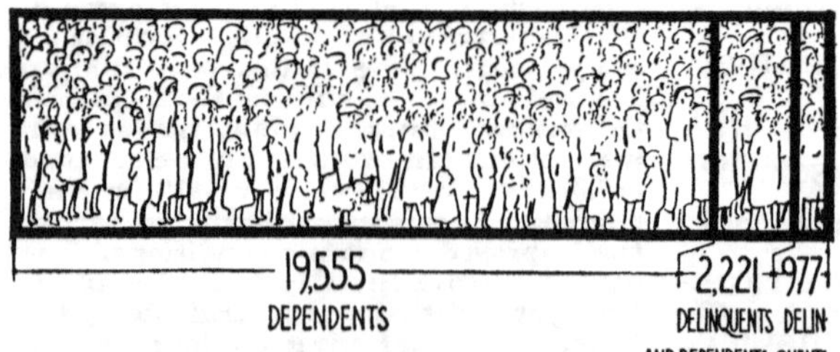

Fig. 25. Nature of institutional care the children supported by the City of New York in private charitable institutions were receiving on January 1, 1916.[17]

There were 22,753 children living in private charitable institutions at public expense at the beginning of 1916. Eighty-six per cent of them (or 19,555) were living in institutions designed solely for dependents and 4 per cent (or 977), in institutions intended for delinquents. Ten per cent (or 2,221) of them were in an institution accommodating both dependents and delinquents.

[21]Source: The Finance Department of the City of New York.

Fig. 26. Some of the city's foster children have their first story hour at the shelter of the Children's Home Bureau.

To hazard one's life on crowded streets in a self-directed search for play is one thing; to be the center of concern of adult play directors is quite another. There are critics who do not believe in directed play, but none of them have visited the shelter of the Children's Home Bureau. Here begins the supervision of the Department of Public Charities over the recreational life of the foster children it places in private homes.

formed this service to an average of fifteen mothers a day. One of the best obstetrical services in the country is at the Greenpoint Hospital. (Fig. 44.) The out-patient department of this institution, opened this year, has been attended by an average of 126 patients daily.

The first metabolic service established in a municipal hospital in New York City was installed during 1916 at the New York City Hospital. This was made possible by a subsidy from private subscribers. Provisions have also been made at this hospital for the accommodation of persons admitted by the courts to the Farm Colony for Inebriates at Warwick, New York, but who

Fig. 27. A bedtime story ends each day's sojourn at the Children's Home Bureau.

A temporary shelter is provided at the Bradford Street Hospital for the city's foster children (between the ages of two and seven) who are waiting to be placed in private homes. Here the children receive mental and physical examinations and, if necessary, clinical and hospital treatment. Here they await the opportunity of the bureau to find a home suitable to their needs. After September, 1917, a similar service will be given at the Children's Clearing Bureau to children over eight years of age who have been approved by the Department of Public Charities for commitment to private charitable institutions.

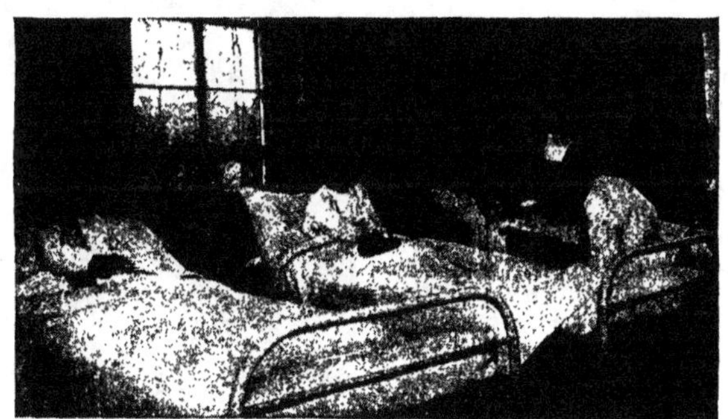

Fig. 28. Before going to their foster homes, charges of the Children's Home Bureau are equipped with an entire new outfit.

Many of the city's foster charges are scantily clad when they come to the Department of Public Charities. Many come from homes where tooth brushes and night clothes are unknown. The department supplies these articles. In this room, many future citizens are made more conscious of the pleasure and responsibility of ownership.

are not physically able to be immediately transferred there. The New York City Hospital claims the best equipped operating suite in the city.

During the recent epidemic of poliomyelitis, the department's hospitals were called into the campaign to combat this disease. The Metropolitan Hospital, which has the largest service for children in the United States, cared for 400 infantile paralysis sufferers. The lowest mortality rate in any institution in the city for patients suffering with this disease was maintained at the New York City Hospital. After the epidemic had subsided, the department purchased eight motor busses to transport patients needing after-care treatment from their homes to the poliomyelitis clinics. (Fig. 46.)

Fig. 29. This American foster home accepted four Italian children for guidance and training.

The Department of Public Charities organized the Children's Home Bureau in June 1916. Owing to the infantile paralysis epidemic of the summer, the actual placement of children in private homes was delayed until October. The intervening period was utilized in investigating some 1,500 private homes which had made application for children. Three hundred and eighty-three of these were approved. During the last three months of the year, 217 children were placed in private homes.

Courtesy of Dr. Carlisle

Fig. 30. The first public hospital in the City of New York was established in 1848.

As early as 1736 provision was made for the care of the sick in the first public almshouse.[22] In an infirmary (about twenty-five by twenty-three feet in dimensions) overlooking Broadway, the city provided six beds for that percentage of its 9,000 population who were at once dependent and ill. The medical officer in charge received £100 ($487.50) a year for his services, out of which he was expected to supply his own medicines. The hospital department was moved to "Belle Vue" with the almshouse in 1816. In 1848, the almshouse was moved to Blackwell's Island and the thirty-two-year-old poorhouse known as "Belle Vue Establishment" became "Belle Vue Hospital" of the Department of Public Charities. In 1867, the Board of Health replaced the "forty incompetent health wardens" who made up the City Inspector's Department. In 1902, the Department of Public Charities and Bellevue and Allied Hospitals became two separate municipal departments. The latter was placed under the control of a board of eight trustees, of which the Commissioner of Public Charities *ex-officio* is a member.

Training schools for nurses are conducted at the Metropolitan, City, Cumberland Street and Kings County Hospitals. (Figs. 47 to 50.) These schools have added important courses to their curricula, designed to give more extensive experience and a broader outlook to their students.

Fig. 31. The New York City Hospital was established in 1857 as the "Island Hospital."

It is at present the oldest hospital under the jurisdiction of the Department of Public Charities.[23] Its lineage may be traced to 1832, when the "Penitentiary Hospital" was opened on Blackwell's Island. On December 15, 1857, it was separated from the penitentiary and called the "Island Hospital." (This name, carved in stone, may still be distinguished high up under the eaves of its administration building.) During a blinding blizzard in the winter of 1858, it was nearly demolished by fire. It was reconstructed and formally opened to the public in 1860. It became the "Charity Hospital" in 1866; and a quarter of a century later (in 1892), the familiar "City Hospital" of the present day. A general hospital with 1,000 beds, this institution has a large maternity service, modernly equipped operating rooms, an active ambulance service (through the Reception Hospital), a pathological laboratory service and a social service department.

---

[22]Robert J. Carlisle, M.D.—An Account of Bellevue Hospital, 1736-1894. Acknowledgment is here made to Dr. Carlisle for much of the historical data presented in connection with the illustrative matter of this report.

[23]Fig. 30, p. 57.

Fig. 32. The Metropolitan Hospital dates back to 1875, when the "New York Homeopathic Hospital" was established on Ward's Island.

It became the Metropolitan Hospital in 1894. In that year it was moved into buildings on Blackwell's Island previously occupied by the insane. In 1902, the last of the insane patients were removed to Ward's Island and the present tuberculosis division was established in the vacated buildings. The hospital maintains a children's division, a leprosy ward and medical and surgical divisions. It is one of the largest general hospitals in the United States.

The Special Hospitals

The Department of Public Charities cared for some 5,500 tuberculous patients at its hospitals during the year. The chief service to them is offered at Sea View Hospital. (Fig. 51.) This institution is one of the world's largest and most costly hospital plants for the treatment of tuberculosis. During the year, 2,401 tuberculous men, women and children were admitted to Sea View Hospital. (Fig. 52.) Forty per cent of these were later dismissed with their disease in a quiescent condition. The Metropolitan Hospital gives similar service to patients suffering from tuberculosis. During 1916, it cared for 150 patients suffering with pulmonary tuberculosis.

The City of New York maintains, under the supervision of the Department of Public Charities, the Central and Neuro-

Fig. 33. The Kings County Hospital was established in 1849.

It was originally the hospital department of the Kings County Almshouse—a small county institution situated over five miles from the present City Hall Park, then known as the "Commons." Today its ambulances answer calls from all parts of the Boroughs of Brooklyn and Queens. It maintains a children's division, a psychopathic service and a service for drug patients committed by the courts. Over 11,000 persons were treated in its dispensaries during 1916. This institution is managed jointly with the Brooklyn Home for the Aged and Infirm. The above building houses the administrative offices of these institutions.

Fig. 34. The Cumberland Street Hospital was opened under the management of the Department of Public Charities in June, 1902.

Prior to 1900, it was operated privately as the Brooklyn Homeopathic Hospital. Located in a community crowded with tenement houses, this hospital has been almost continually taxed to capacity. During 1916, dispensary treatment was given here to 21,221 persons. Dental and pre-natal clinics have been established here during the past year. On December 27, 1916, $600,000 was appropriated for a new building for this hospital.[24]

Fig. 35. The Coney Island Hospital was established on May 18, 1910.

Prior to 1910, the hospital facilities available to the crowds who visited the world's unique Coney Island and its neighboring resorts were limited to three small buildings on Sea Breeze Avenue. These were known as the "Reception Hospital." This institution provided only emergency service. Patients in need of prolonged treatment were transferred to the Kings County Hospital. Today, the Coney Island Hospital of the Department of Public Charities serves this district.

logical Hospital on Blackwell's Island for the specialized care of patients suffering from nervous diseases. (Fig. 53.) There were cared for at this institution during 1916, 2,830 patients, most of whom were beyond middle age. During the year, the management of

Fig. 36. The Greenpoint Hospital was established in 1915.

The Department of Public Charities met the need for a public hospital in the crowded Greenpoint section of Brooklyn when this modern institution was opened on October 25, 1915. The hospital has been enthusiastically accepted by the community which it serves. The dispensary, opened in 1916, has already outgrown its original quarters.

[24]Fig. 104, p. 116.

Fig. 37. The Bradford Street Hospital was established on November 25, 1902.

This hospital was originally opened as an emergency ambulance station of the Kings County Hospital. In 1916, it was changed to a dispensary and general clinic. In the latter months of the year, the upper floor was converted into the shelter of the Children's Home Bureau.[25]

this institution was placed under the supervision of the New York City Hospital. It had been previously allied with the New York City Home for the Aged and Infirm. Occupational work has become an important feature of this institution's treatment. In place of long lines of patients sitting with idle hands day by day, endlessly thinking, groups of men and women may be seen working at basket-making, rug and toy-making, knitting and crocheting.

Social Service in the Hospitals

In seven of the hospitals under the supervision of the Department of Public Charities, social after-care of patients forms an important part of their treatment. Social workers are affiliated with the City, Metropolitan, and Central and Neurological

Fig. 38. The Pelham Bay Home was opened by the Department of Public Charities on August 19, 1913, as the "Hunter's Island Convalescent Home."

Here is housed the first convalescent home of the Department of Public Charities. Mothers and babies are here received for recuperation after illness. This building has watched history in the making. It withstood an attack by the enemy in the War of 1812. It was used as a shelter for wounded soldiers in the Spanish-American War. It has been the property of the city for about twenty years. This department secured its use from the park department in 1913.

[25]Fig. 27, p. 55.

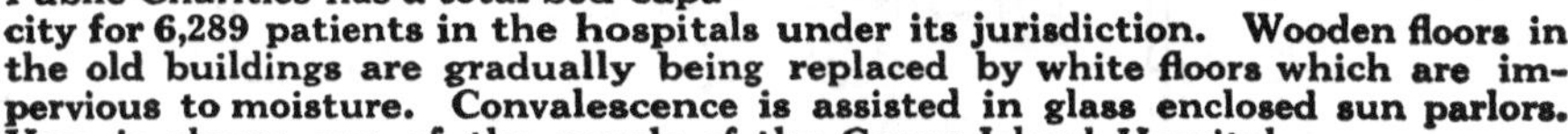

Fig. 39. In restoring the health of their patients, light, air and cleanliness are the first aids of the hospitals of the Department of Public Charities.

History reports that the early hospitals of the department were so crowded that men and women were sometimes herded in the same ward. "Hospital odor" was a familiar phrase aptly describing existing conditions. Today, "surgically clean" is the byword and hospital wards are white, wide and airy. The Department of Public Charities has a total bed capacity for 6,289 patients in the hospitals under its jurisdiction. Wooden floors in the old buildings are gradually being replaced by white floors which are impervious to moisture. Convalescence is assisted in glass enclosed sun parlors. Here is shown one of the wards of the Coney Island Hospital.

Hospitals on Blackwell's Island; the Kings County, Cumberland Street, and Greenpoint Hospitals in Brooklyn, and at the

Fig. 40. The X-ray is an indispensable ally to the hospitals of the Department of Public Charities.

Discovered in 1895, by William Konrad Röntgen of Würzberg, Germany, the X-ray has given second sight to physicians and surgeons the world over. By the use of these powerful rays, the physician can see through the human body, watch the beating of the heart, locate bone fractures, and trace the root canals of decaying teeth. He can more accurately diagnose obscure conditions. He can treat cancerous growths. At the Kings County Hospital, 5,844 radiographs were made during 1916. This was an average of sixteen a day. Electrical treatment was given by this hospital to 1,219 patients during the year.

Sea View Hospital on Staten Island. This work is under the general supervision of the Bureau of Social Investigations.

The social workers' efforts supplement those of the phy-

Fig. 41. The remedial value of nutritious foods is not underestimated in the special diet kitchens of the Department of Public Charities' hospitals.

During 1916, the Department of Public Charities fed an average of 15,716 persons daily, in its institutions. The departmental steward supervises the purchase, distribution and service of food in these hospitals and homes. There are in the department's hospitals several special diet kitchens similar to this one at the Metropolitan Hospital.

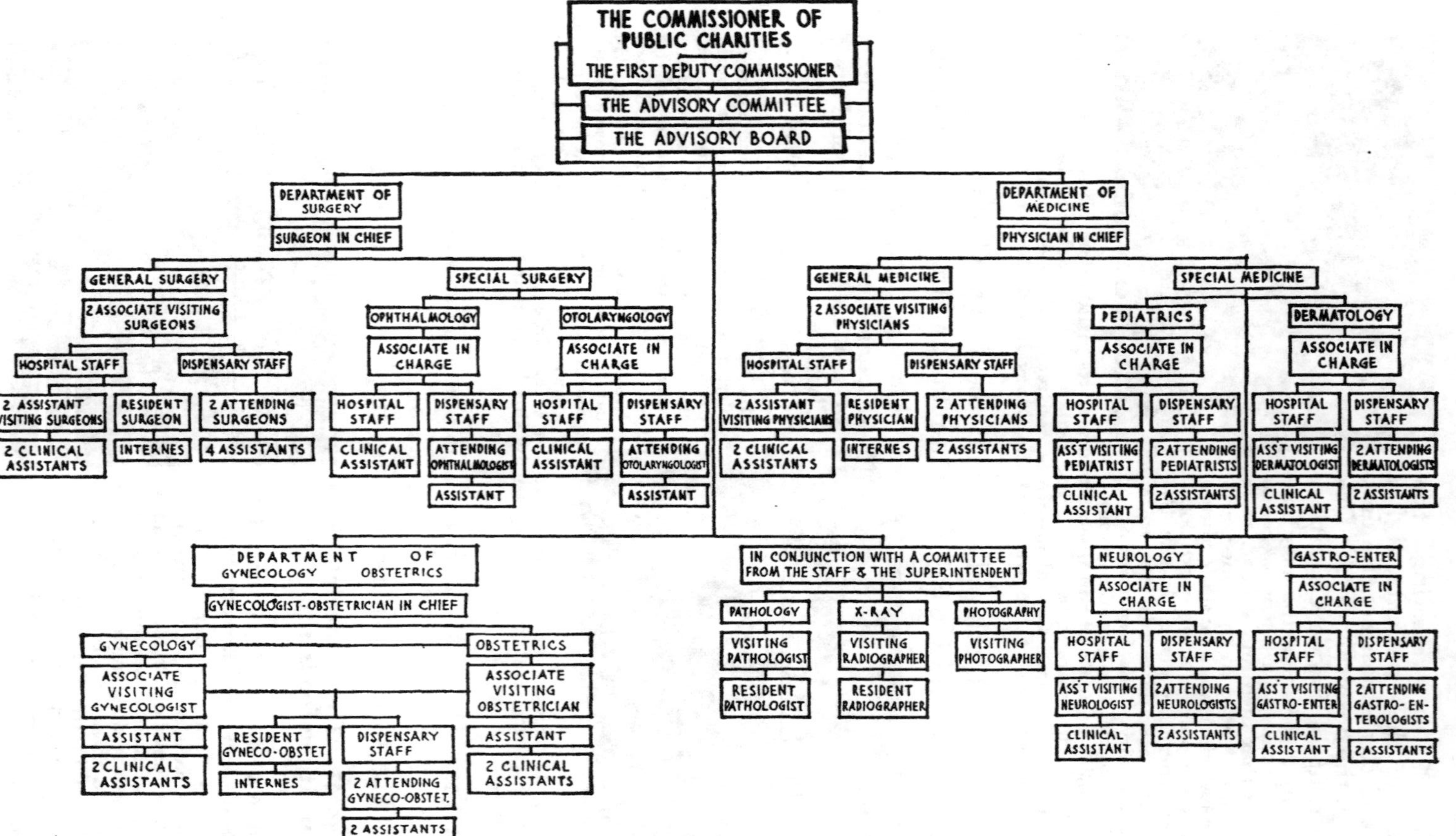

Fig. 42. The organization of the Greenpoint Hospital.

This plan of organization was modelled after the scheme of management existing in two of the foremost hospitals in America—the Johns Hopkins, and the Massachusetts General Hospitals. In 1916, the Cumberland Street Hospital was reorganized after this plan.

sicians and nurses in the hospitals. They attempt to remedy those abnormalities in the patients' social life which often present the greatest barriers to their physical health. They assist the discharged patient to re-establish himself upon leaving the hos-

Fig. 43. The Reception Hospital was established in 1911.

Since May 1, 1911, this one story building has housed the only public hospital in the thickly populated district adjoining 70th Street and the East River. This hospital is open day and night for the emergency treatment of patients. Applicants for admission to the department's hospitals on Blackwell's Island are examined here.

pital, drawing upon the countless resources of the private charitable agencies. (Fig. 54.)

During 1916, many persons were aided by these departments. Men and women were frequently found employment who had been unemployed over a long period of sickness. Often persons were aided in making a difficult change in vocation to adjust their manner of earning a livelihood to a physical disability. It was necessary to assist many such who were victims of accident or of diseases brought on by their work.

In visiting patients' homes, these workers often acted as instructors in housekeeping. Mothers were taught important lessons in child care. Instruction was often given in the purchasing

Fig. 44. Their maternity services are a distinct feature of the hospitals of the Department of Public Charities.

Berlin has established a hospital solely for the reduction of infant mortality. The municipal hospitals of New York City are fast learning that many infantile diseases are preventable, if mothers are instructed in child care before and after their babies are born. One of the activities of the Department of Health is designed for this purpose. The New York City and Metropolitan Hospitals of the Department of Public Charities have large maternity services. The model maternity building of the former was planned in 1888 by Henry J. Garrigues, M.D., the man who first introduced antiseptic methods into midwifery. The Cumberland Street Hospital maintains a pre-natal clinic; and the Kings County and Greenpoint Hospitals obstetrical clinics. This is a view of the maternity ward in the Greenpoint Hospital.

Fig. 45. The curative value of modern surgery is demonstrated daily in the operating rooms of the Department of Public Charities.

The New York City Hospital now boasts of a $50,000 operating suite, acknowledged by experts to be among the finest in the United States. During 1916, its four operating theatres were completely equipped. There were provided surgeons' and nurses' robing rooms, anesthesia and sterilizing rooms. During 1916, 872 operations were performed at this hospital. Surgical treatment was given to 1,564 patients

and preparation of foods. The activities of a worker at one of the hospitals brought about a reconciliation between a husband

Fig. 46. An infantile paralysis bus at one of the after-care clinics of the Department of Public Charities.

The epidemic which claimed 2,448 lives in New York City in 1916 left 6,575 patients in need of after-care. Twelve busses of the Department of Public Charities transport patients to after-care clinics. Each bus is in charge of a nurse. This service is maintained between two clinics in the Bronx, five in Brooklyn, six in Manhattan and three in Queens. Some 500 sufferers are benefited.

and wife. This service was rendered by teaching the woman methods of cleanliness and personal hygiene.

Fig. 47. The Metropolitan Hospital Training School for Nurses was established in 1892.

Until 1902, this school was under the administration of the superintendent of the Metropolitan Hospital. Since that date, it has been under the direction of a separate board of managers. The school offers a three years' course. Its pupils are afforded a varied experience. Opportunity is provided for study in the social service department of the hospital. The building here shown was erected in 1909.

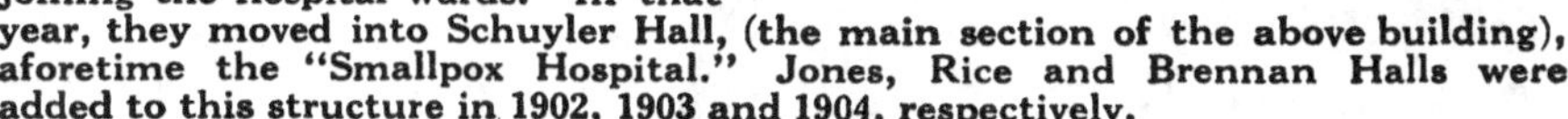

Fig. 48. The City Hospital School of Nursing was established on October 1, 1875, as the Charity Hospital Training School for Nurses.

It was opened two years after the Department of Public Charities established at Bellevue Hospital the pioneer nurses training school of America, the "New York Training School for Nurses." It is at present the oldest school under the department's jurisdiction. Until 1866, the pupils were quartered in rooms adjoining the hospital wards. In that year, they moved into Schuyler Hall, (the main section of the above building), aforetime the "Smallpox Hospital." Jones, Rice and Brennan Halls were added to this structure in 1902, 1903 and 1904, respectively.

Patients with no friends or relatives able to call for them were taken to their homes or accompanied to trains. Diagnosis and treatment was often secured from specialists. A page from the annual record of a worker at one of the hospitals, records among a list of some twenty-six distinct services, 6,570 ward interviews, 3,136 visits of patients to the office, 1,148 letters written, and 609 visits to institutions and homes.

Fig. 49. The Cumberland Street Hospital Training School for Nurses was organized in 1902.

Organized jointly with the Cumberland Street Hospital, this school enrolled sixteen pupils during its first year of existence. Two private residences near the hospital now serve as a home for the nurses. With the completion of the new Cumberland Street Hospital[19] the school will enter upon a wider field of service.

Fig. 50. The Kings County Hospital Training School for Nurses was established in October 1897.

This modern building, completed in 1912, houses the largest nurses' training school in Brooklyn. Because of its connection with the Kings County Hospital, which registered some 28,000 patients in its wards and dispensaries in 1916, the school presents a wide opportunity for experience and study.

Fig. 51. The Sea View Hospital was established on October 28, 1913.

It is the only hospital in New York City caring solely for tubercular patients. It is built on the group plan and at present provides beds for 763 patients.[26] It was built on the highest part of Staten Island overlooking the Narrows in recognition of the advantages of the open air treatment for tuberculosis — the disease which is responsible for one in every seven deaths occurring in New York City. Forty per cent of the 2,401 tubercular men, women and children admitted to this hospital in 1916 were discharged with their disease in a quiescent condition.

Providing Convalescent Care

The department maintains for the City of New York a convalescent home for mothers and babies on Hunter's Island. During the year, the name of this institution has been changed

Fig. 52. Tubercular patients receive an abundance of light and air at the Sea View Hospital.

At this hospital the Department of Public Charities accepts patients suffering with moderately advanced tuberculosis. During 1916, 2,401 patients were treated here. The department maintains a similar service for tubercular patients at the Metropolitan Hospital.

Fig. 53. The Central and Neurological Hospital was established as a separate hospital in 1916.

In 1867, a hospital for incurables was erected near the almshouse. Until 1916, this had been a hospital ward of the New York City Home for the Aged and Infirm where the incurables were quartered and treated. Today, it is administered as a separate hospital unit under the supervision of the medical superintendent of the New York City Hospital. Here are treated neurotic disorders, gout, rheumatism, and the many industrial diseases of the aged poor. Extensive use has been made at this institution of occupational therapy.[27] During 1916, 2,830 patients were treated here.

---

[26]Figs. 113-115. [27]Fig. 56, p. 67.

Fig. 54. Social after-care re-enforces medical treatment in hospitals of the Department of Public Charities.

Where the physician's work ends, the task of the social worker begins. For the countless services which the busy specialist cannot perform and which the poor so seldom have friend or relative to perform, the patient must seek the aid of the hospital social service department. In 1911, there were only two such departments in the hospitals of the Department of Public Charities. To-day, there are seven. Similar services are provided at the department's shelters, at the hospital and school for the feebleminded and at the mortuary.

from the "Hunter's Island Home for Convalescent Mothers and Babies" to "The Pelham Bay Home." (Fig. 38.) Here, women of all ages, without regard to race, creed, or color, who are not strong enough to return to work, and who cannot pay for needed rest, are cared for by the city for an average period of three weeks. During 1916, 579 mothers and their babies were given care. (Fig. 55.) Charitable agencies and maternity hospitals referred the women to the home where they were given nourishing food and taught how to care for and feed their babies. Most of the patients are unmarried mothers of about twenty-one years, who were formerly self-supporting.

Occupational Work Among Patients and Dependents

Recently, a medical examination was made of 500 residents at the New York City Home for the Aged and Infirm. Fifty-nine per cent of them were adjudged able to work. The other 41 per cent were sick or infirm. Many of the latter were ca-

Fig. 55. A basket of Pelham Bay Home babies.

A fortnight of sun, air and healthful sleep at the Pelham Bay Home is an excellent start in life for these babies. A visiting physician watches their physical condition during their stay. Their mothers are instructed in baby welfare.

Fig. 56. In hospitals of the Department of Public Charities busy hands divert the minds of convalescent patients from their ills.

In March, 1916, the commissioner of charities appointed a committee to organize occupational work among the chronic patients and residents in the department's hospitals and homes. Under the direction of this committee, many men and women, formerly idle, listless and morose, have become producers of articles which have a distinct commercial value. Already tennis nets made by tuberculous patients are pronounced salable by several New York City business houses. Work as a curative factor in the treatment of sickness seems first to have been advocated in the Pennsylvania Hospital, but the modern science of occupational therapy is scarcely ten years old.[28]

pable, however, of contributing to their own support. Residents of the homes have always helped to do the necessary work about these institutions. But when this work was too heavy for those partially handicapped, they were forced to sit in idleness. In March, 1916, with the aid of the New York City Visiting Committee, the department appointed a director of occupations and two teachers to organize work for these dependents. Teachers were also se-

Fig. 57. Sheltered from the competition of modern industry, these aged wards of the Department of Public Charities glory that their useful abilities have not entirely waned.

This cheerful group of workers at the New York City Home for the Aged and Infirm presents a convincing argument for occupational therapy. The Department of Public Charities plans to develop manual training in its institutions. By thoughtful selection of materials and careful supervision, work which has an economic as well as a therapeutic value can be provided. The department's director of occupations has expressed the need for additional space in the various institutions for the development of this work.[29]

---

[28]William Rush Dunton, Pr.—History of Occupational Therapy, The Modern Hospital, June 1917, p. 380.

[29]Susan C. Johnson, Occupational Therapy in New York City Institutions, The Modern Hospital, June 1917, p. 414.

cured for part time work at the Metropolitan and Sea View Hospitals.

In a short time, it was demonstrated that, with proper training and supervision, these persons could make a substantial contribution to their own support. Many patients in the department's hospitals and homes are now making salable articles. (Figs. 56 and 57.)

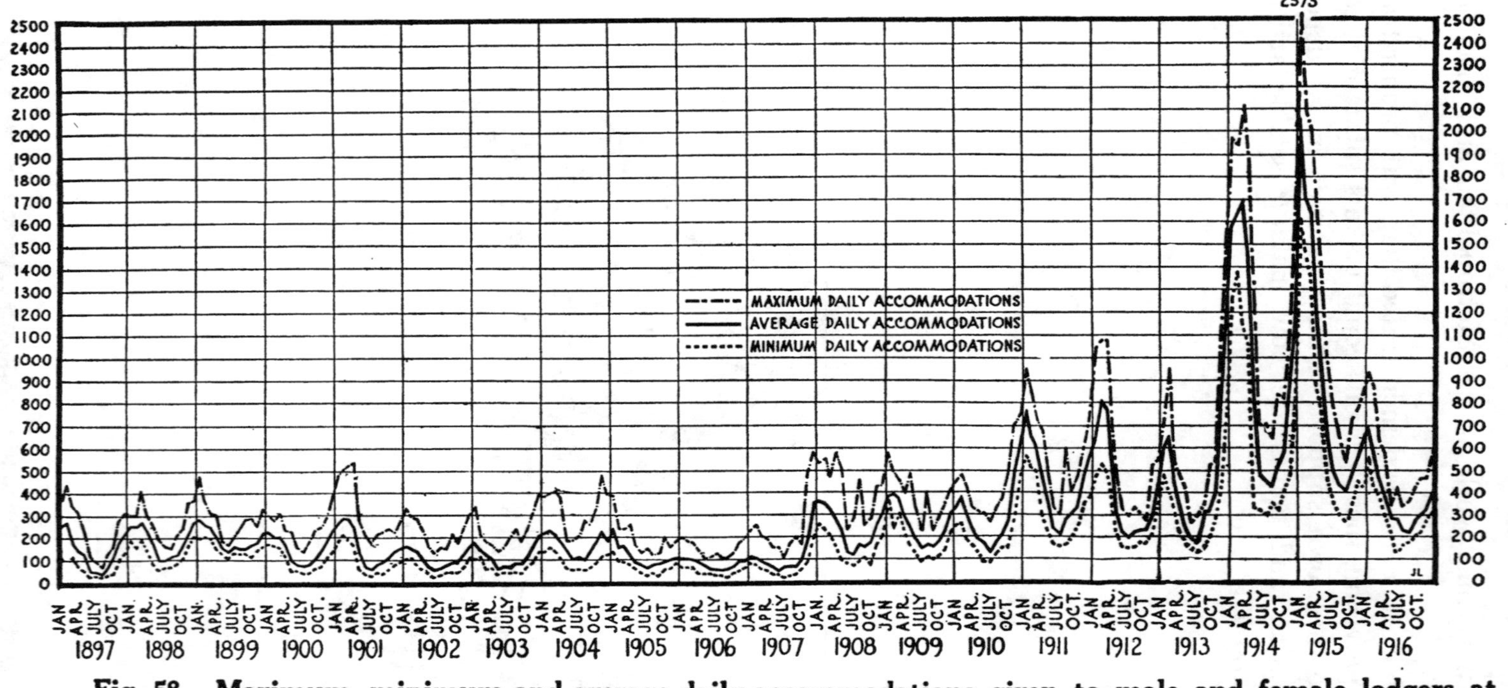

Fig. 58. Maximum, minimum and average daily accommodations given to male and female lodgers at the Municipal Lodging House by the month, 1897-1916, inclusive.

The census curve of the Municipal Lodging House reflects with some fidelity the ebb and flow of the labor demand. Obviously, the ratio of men to jobs is greater in winter than in summer. The winter peaks form in themselves a secondary curve which varies from year to year with the general industrial conditions. The lowest registration since the establishment of the Municipal Lodging House was on June 15, 1897, when forty persons were accommodated. From the comparatively prosperous year of 1906 the number of applicants grew until in the winter of 1913-14 an unprecedented situation occurred. The following winter marked another growth. In November, the situation became serious. In December, it became critical. January 3, 1915, marked the highest registration in the history of the Municipal Lodging House. On that night, 2,573 lodgers were given accommodations.

THE CARE OF THE HOMELESS

The City's Shelters for the Homeless

THE problem of sheltering annually hundreds of destitute homeless persons is perhaps inherent in the size of New York City. The stranger who is left penniless by some unfortunate circumstance--and there are scores of such annually--must be sheltered. The man or woman who is suddenly thrown out of employment without means for self-support must be cared for. The less fit members of the community, who are more often out of work than at work, must have some home. The aged citizen who has contributed his resources in building up this community must be provided for when his labor capital has been exhausted. Citizens some years ago found it undesirable to require these to sleep on a park bench, in some dark hallway, or on one of the various docks along the water fronts. For their temporary care, the City of New York, under the Department of Public Charities, operates the Municipal Lodging House. For their specialized and permanent care, the city operates the New York City Farm Colony, the New York City Home for the Aged and Infirm, and the Brooklyn Home for the Aged and Infirm. (Fig. 59.)

The winters of suffering brought on by the industrial depression of 1914 and 1915 presented an unprecedented demand on the Department of Public Charities for the housing of the homeless. Largely as a result of the war in Europe, the department during these years was compelled to care for, in its public institutions alone, a daily average of over 2,000 more people than in 1913, which up to that time was the largest number ever cared for in the history of the city. (Fig. 58.) Without any material cost to the city for new buildings, however, shelter and beds were provided to meet this abnormal demand. A total added winter capacity of 2,300 beds was secured. By studied readjustment of the space in existing buildings, more than 1,000 beds were added to the capacity of the department's institutions. An additional 1,500 beds as an annex to the Municipal Lodging House were

THE CARE OF THE DESTITUTE HOMELESS

THE TEMPORARY SHELTER

THE MUNICIPAL LODGING HOUSE
432 E. 25TH ST MANHATTAN

THE TEMPORARY ACCOMODATION OF DESTITUTE LODGERS.

THE TEMPORARY & PERMANENT SHELTER

THE SEA VIEW FARMS
(FORMERLY THE N.Y.C. FARM COLONY)
CASTLETON CORNERS
STATEN ISLAND

THE TEMPORARY AND PERMANENT ACCOMODATION OF DESTITUTE SEMI-ABLE-BODIED MEN, OF DEPENDENT AGED COUPLES, AND OF SINGLE WOMEN (PROVIDES ALSO A SANATORIUM AND PSYCOPATIC SERVICE)

THE BROOKLYN HOME FOR THE AGED & INFIRM
CLARKSON AND NEW YORK AVES.
BROOKLYN

THE TEMPORARY AND PERMANENT ACCOMODATION OF AGED AND INFIRM PERSONS, INCLUDING THE BLIND AND PARALYTIC.
(MANAGED JOINTLY WITH KINGS COUNTY HOSPITAL)

THE N.Y.C. HOME FOR THE AGED & INFIRM
BLACKWELLS ISLAND

THE TEMPORARY AND PERMANENT ACCOMODATION OF AGED AND INFIRM PERSONS, INCLUDING THE BLIND AND PARALYTIC.

JL

Fig. 59. Organization of the activities in the Department of Public Charities for the care of the homeless.

The department's shelters offer an aggregate of over 6,200 beds to the homeless. An aggregate of 152,653 accommodations were given to persons at these institutions in 1916. At these homes, society's misfits are often restored to a partial earning capacity, and placed in outside employment.

provided on the East Twenty-fourth Street recreation pier. At the New York City Home for the Aged and Infirm, 120 additional beds were provided. Had these and other facilities been secured by constructing new buildings, an appropriation of approximately $800,000 would have been necessary.

The City's Temporary Shelter for the Homeless

The Municipal Lodging House has six light, airy sleeping rooms; double deck, white enamel beds; shower baths, a formaldehyde fumigating plant, a dining-room and a laundry. It pro-

Fig. 60. The Municipal Lodging House was established in 1896.

It was first opened at 398 First Avenue, Manhattan, with a bed capacity for 317 lodgers. The building here shown was opened in February 1909. It has normal accommodations for approximately 1,000 homeless persons. It has six light, airy sleeping rooms (one of which is equipped for the accommodation of women and children), white enamel beds, shower baths, a formaldehyde fumigating plant, a dining-room and a laundry. It houses employment and social service bureaus and a medical and a dental clinic. It is one of America's best equipped lodging house buildings.

vides a medical clinic, a dental clinic and a free employment bureau. (Fig. 60.) A social investigator from the Bureau of Social Investigations is stationed at the institution. Dispossessed families, mothers with babies, the sick and the aged are given special care there. (Fig. 62.)

An aggregate of 141,859 accommodations were given to destitute homeless persons at the Municipal Lodging House in 1916. To say that the persons receiving these services were for the time without shelter, money or friends does not adequately describe them. They were as heterogenous a mass of humanity as one would expect to comb from the slums of New York, Chicago, Dublin, Petrograd, Alexandria or

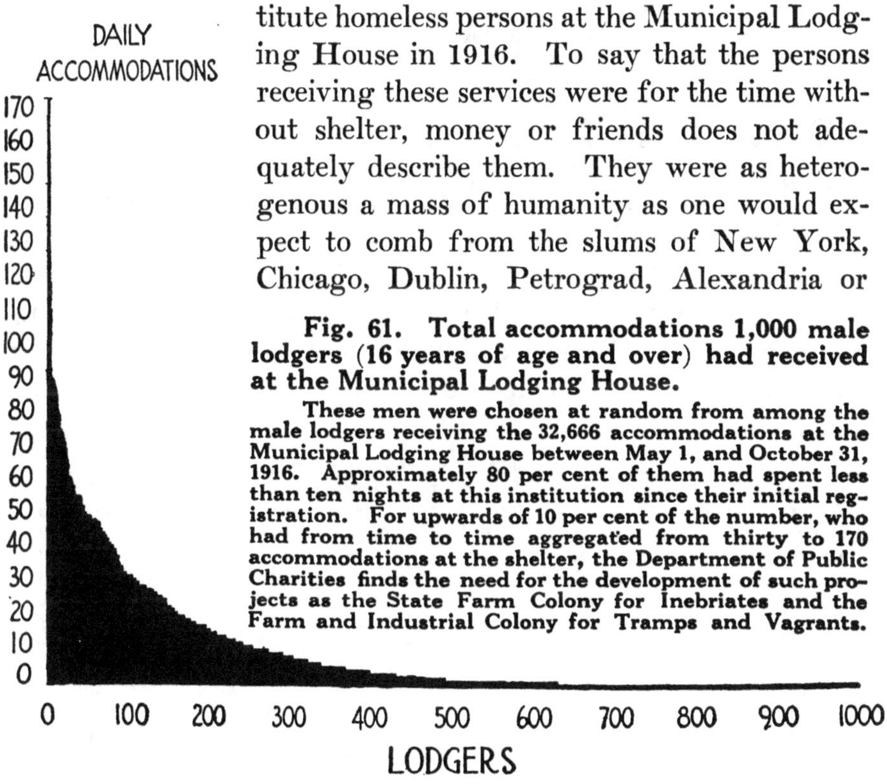

DAILY ACCOMMODATIONS
170 160 150 140 130 120 110 100 90 80 70 60 50 40 30 20 10 0
0 100 200 300 400 500 600 700 800 900 1000
LODGERS

Fig. 61. Total accommodations 1,000 male lodgers (16 years of age and over) had received at the Municipal Lodging House.

These men were chosen at random from among the male lodgers receiving the 32,666 accommodations at the Municipal Lodging House between May 1, and October 31, 1916. Approximately 80 per cent of them had spent less than ten nights at this institution since their initial registration. For upwards of 10 per cent of the number, who had from time to time aggregated from thirty to 170 accommodations at the shelter, the Department of Public Charities finds the need for the development of such projects as the State Farm Colony for Inebriates and the Farm and Industrial Colony for Tramps and Vagrants.

San Juan, from a quaint secluded hamlet in the Tyrolian Alps, a frontier lumbering camp in far Western Canada, a prominent mining town in the coal fields of Pennslyvania, or an isolated dwelling in a middle west prairie. They were from all lands, all circumstances and all conditions of civilized society. (Fig. 63.)

Fig. 62. Many people do not know that women and children are accommodated temporarily at the Municipal Lodging House.

The Department of Public Charities has provided temporary accommodations for women and children since 1896, when the first Municipal Lodging House was established. During 1916, 11,612 accommodations were given to women at the Municipal Lodging House. Accommodations were given to 2,839 children under six years of age. The employment bureau secured 3,905 situations for women, during this year.

It is probable that no other institution in the land is more sensitive to changes in the labor market than the Municipal Lodging House. A continuous ebb and flow in the number of its applicants goes on, from day to day, from season to season and from one year to another. (Figs. 64 and 65.) The norm of these variations follows closely the changes in industrial prosperity.[30]

During such periods of industrial depression as occurred in the winter of 1914-1915, the beds of the lodging house are filled largely by men who are usually employed and self-supporting.[31] As the demand diminishes they are thrown out of work. As their savings diminish, they take refuge in this shelter. These individuals, for whom the experience of unemployment is a common one, form a residue of dependents

[30]The population of the Municipal Lodging House does not in all probability show so high a ratio of change as the index of general unemployment would show. This follows from its varied composition. Not only is the total number of applicants continuously changing, but the relative importance of the various elements within the population is continually fluctuating. It has been possible to gauge this continuous change in the constituency of the lodging house group only in a general way. It was not until November 1, 1916, that cards were numbered serially, so that the number of individuals, as well as the number of registrations, could be ascertained. A lodger's social status, therefore, has made its impression on the general constituency of the registered population for the year as often as he returned for lodgings. Perhaps a single German contributed to the relative importance of Germans in the annual population census as many as thirty or forty times, or as often as he had registered at the institution during the year. It has been necessary, therefore, to supplement with experience and observation the analysis of aggregates which have been thus vitiated by the repetition of certain of their component factors.

which requires the operation of a municipal shelter year in and year out. (Fig. 61.)

The restoration of normal industrial conditions has radically altered the problems of management at the Municipal Lodging House. The sudden approach and intensity of the crisis of 1914 and 1915 required action that was at once quick and on a large scale -- action which was spectacular. It was necessarily unstudied, and therefore frequently crude and unscientific. The Department of Public Charities has directed its efforts during 1916 towards a quiet, nonspectacular carrying out of its program to make the lodging house a human repair shop, manned and equipped to rebuild the lives of the poor unfortunate homeless who enter its doors for shelter and care.

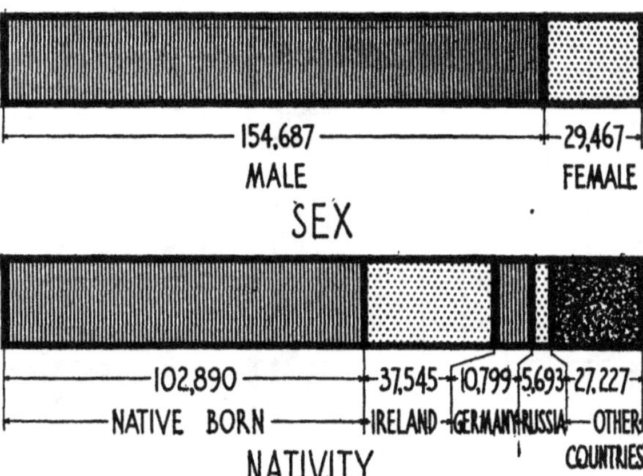

Fig. 63. Sex and nativity of the 184,154 dependents receiving accommodations at various institutions of the Department of Public Charities during the year ending December 31, 1916.[32]

The year's applicants to nine institutions (seven hospitals and two homes) are represented in this chart. Eighty-three out of every hundred applicants were males, and fifty-five out of every hundred were native born. 77 per cent (or 141,859) of the applicants here represented had been registered at the Municipal Lodging House. But the composition and characteristics of its lodgers are not unlike those registered at the other institutions here represented.

So far as possible, some work has been required from all lodgers who are physically and mentally capable of performing it, and who have not had paid employment to which they might go. (Figs. 66 and 67.) This labor has been performed, not as

[31]This assertion was borne out in a study of 2,000 men who applied at the Municipal Lodging House for shelter during March, 1914—at a time when the labor market was just beginning to become more normal, following the marked depression of the previous winter. A large number of these men were dependent primarily because of current industrial conditions, and not through faults or handicaps of their own. Another group were unemployable, permanently or temporarily, and would have been regardless of the conditions of industry. "The Men We Lodge", *Robert Bertrand Brown* , a report of the Advisory Social Service Committee of the Municipal Lodging House. The Department of Public Charities, City of New York, 1915, pp. 11-20.

[32]The Annual Report of the Department of Public Charities for the year ending December 31, 1916. Addenda, Social Statistics, A. Table 3.

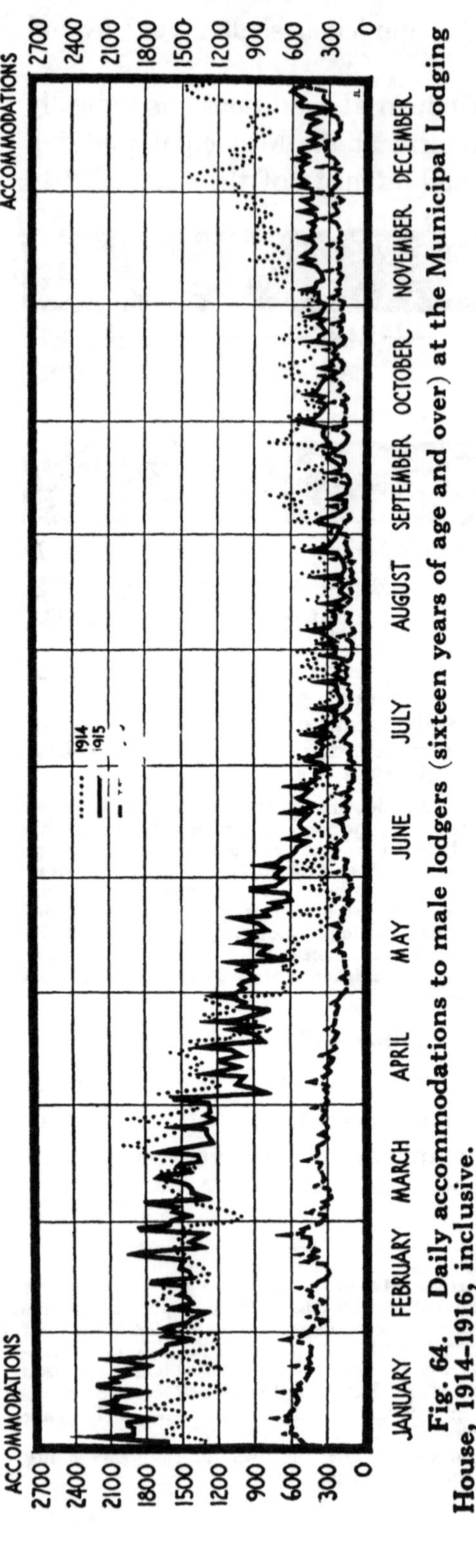

Fig. 64. Daily accommodations to male lodgers (sixteen years of age and over) at the Municipal Lodging House, 1914–1916, inclusive.

The passing of the recent unemployment crisis was as rapid and as well defined as its approach. The registrations of male applicants at the Municipal Lodging House decreased from over 2,400 in January, 1915, to less than 400 in July of the same year. During 1916, the highest daily census of male lodgers was on January 8, when 796 were accommodated; the lowest was on June 30, when 78 were accommodated. That Saturday night is a traditional bath night and that lodgers are required to do a minimum amount of work on Sunday morning is the explanation of the sharp turns in the curves, which occur with strict regularity on every seventh day.

a work test, but in the nature of repayment to the institution and the city for the benefits which each individual has received. Lodgers were informed that four hours' work per day or twenty-four hours' work per week would pay for their accommodation in the house. Unless they chose otherwise, each would be assigned to eight hours' work on alternate days, making it possible for him to look for work on the remaining days of his stay. During the year, the lodging house employment bureau placed an aggregate of 3,905 lodgers in jobs.

The practice of requiring all applicants for lodging at the institution to have a physical examination upon registration has continued throughout the year. (Fig. 69.) During the nine months ending December 31, 1916, there were 233 destitute homeless persons who were admitted to tuberculosis hospitals through the instrumentality of the lodging house. A free dental clinic for lodgers, the first of its kind in the United States, has been established in connection with the medical department of the shelter. (Fig. 68.)

The City's Permanent Shelters for the Homeless

Dependent aged couples and partially disabled men are sheltered at the New York City Farm Colony. The farm affords comfortable dormitory quarters and outdoor life to its residents. (Fig. 70.) In many respects, the make-up of its population is similar to that of the Municipal Lodging House, since a large proportion of the colonists are transferred from the latter

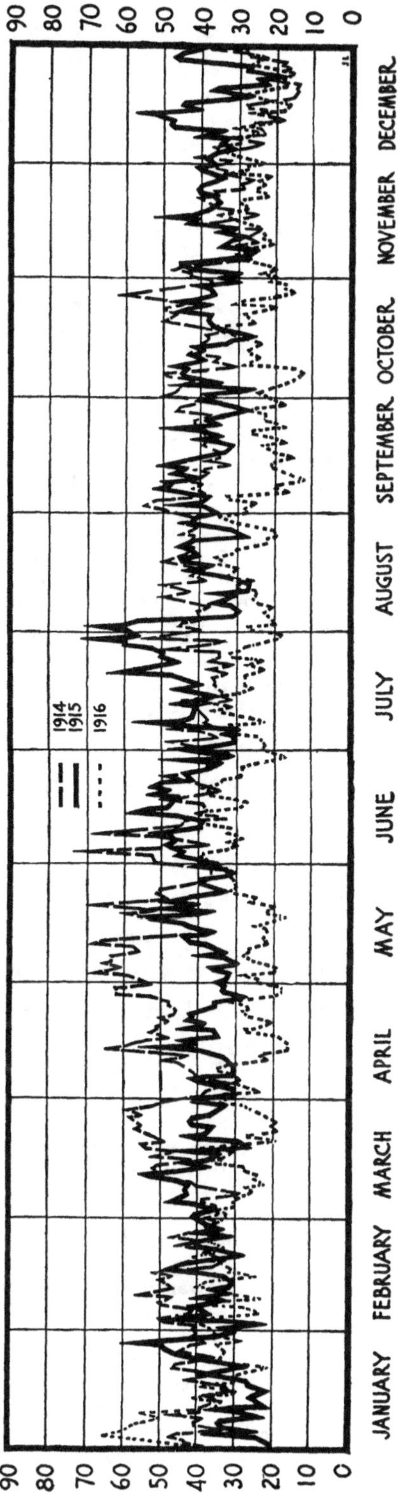

Fig. 65. Daily accommodations to female lodgers (sixteen years of age and over) at the Municipal Lodging House, 1914-1916, inclusive.

Homeless men and homeless women present two distinct and almost wholly dissimilar problems. The difference is partially shown in a study of the census curves of the Municipal Lodging House. Rarely is the census of men less than 100. Rarely does the registration of women exceed seventy-five. The census of the men, following the labor market, expands in the winter and contracts in the summer. There is no such ready explanation of the sporadic fluctuation of the women's census. It reveals one thing certainly—that the causes which produce homelessness among women are different in nature and in time of occurrence from those which produce homelessness among men. During 1916, the highest daily census of women lodgers at the Municipal Lodging House was on January 4, when sixty-five were accommodated; the lowest was on September 9 and on October 7, when twelve were accommodated.

Fig. 66. Constant application is necessary to maintain the desired standard of cleanliness and comfort in institutions of the Department of Public Charities.

In the department's shelters, this work is largely performed by the residents. The policy of requiring labor from the able-bodied dependents enables them to partially repay the city for their accommodations. Moreover, it protects the city from the unreasonable demands of the rounder. These men are "doing their bit" in return for shelter at the Municipal Lodging House.

institution. During the industrial depression of 1914 and 1915, many able-bodied men were forced to enter the farm colony for temporary shelter. The nature of the population has changed with the return to prosperous conditions of industry. During 1916, a large number of the colony's residents have been temporarily incapacitated. Perhaps due to its proximity to Sea View Hospital, the colony aids many tubercular patients whose diseases have been arrested. Here, such patients are given light work and sufficient exercise to assist them to regain their physical endurance. Similar service is rendered to many men suffering with alcoholism.

But for the accommodations offered at this institution during 1916, sixteen aged couples would have been compelled to separate. At the farm colony, cottages are provided, where old persons may keep intact the association which they have had through years of married life. Two new cottages were opened during 1916, affording additional accommodations for thirty-five more couples.

Fig. 67. Applicants who are physically and mentally capable are required to do some work in return for their accommodation at the shelters of the Department of Public Charities.

Here, men from the Municipal Lodging House are baling and loading waste paper on the pier at the foot of East Twenty-six Street. Unless incapacitated or excused for outside employment, lodgers at this institution are required to give four hours of work in return for their accommodation. If they desire, they are assigned to work eight hours on alternate days so that they may look for work in the intervening time.

Every resident at the New York City Farm Colony is given some form of productive work. During 1916, the colony's truck farm has continued to supply outdoor work to men physically able to profit thereby. (Fig. 72.) When it was believed that a man would profit more by indoor work, he was engaged in one of several industrial activities within the institution. The colonists produced 712 mattresses, 681 rag rugs, 346 pillows and 299 rope mats, during the year. Fifty-five tons of hay and four tons of straw were harvested. Striking economies continued to result from the raising of vegetables here for the department's tables. Over 72,000 pounds of pork were produced during the year. (Fig. 71.)

Fig. 68. The free dental clinic opened at the Municipal Lodging House during 1916 was the first to be established in a public philanthropic shelter in the United States.

Since October 1916, a dental clinic has been maintained at the lodging house through the voluntary services of student dentists. The dental service is optional with the lodger. During the first month of the clinic's existence, over 250 applicants received dental treatment.

For homeless persons who are likely to be permanently unemployed, the City of New York maintains under the Department of Public Charities two homes--the New York City Home for the Aged and Infirm on Blackwell's Island and the Brooklyn Home for the Aged and Infirm on Clarkson Street near Albany Avenue. (Figs. 74 and 75.) During 1916, fewer young and

Fig. 69. The Municipal Lodging House is a door of entry to clinical and hospital treatment for hundreds of its applicants.

Before being assigned to a bed, each applicant for shelter at the Municipal Lodging House is required to submit to a physical examination. Two physicians are in charge of the above clinic. Here minor ailments are treated. Hospital treatment is secured for persons who require it. Contagious diseases are apprehended. During the last nine months of 1916, 233 homeless persons were sent to tuberculosis hospitals from the Municipal Lodging House. A separate examination room is maintained for women and children.

Fig. 70. The New York City Farm Colony was established in 1902.

Its buildings are erected on the site of the old Richmond County Almshouse. Originally comprising only ninety-eight acres, the New York City Farm Colony, jointly with Sea View Hospital, now covers 320 acres. During 1916, 1,315 men were sheltered at the colony. Two new cottages have been made available recently at this institution to provide shelter for destitute old married couples.

able-bodied men and women were harbored in these homes. This was largely due, of course, to the better industrial conditions existing in the city and in the outlying districts. Few who were willing and able to work have failed to obtain jobs.

For the first time in its history, the New York City Home for the Aged and Infirm was this year lighted with electricity. Two vacant cottages accommodating sixteen attendants have been thoroughly renovated. The nurses' home has been completed during 1916. Sixty-eight sleeping rooms and a reception room were furnished anew, making it possible for each nurse to have a room to herself. The porch in the rear of two of the wards has been enclosed in glass and fixtures for their heating are now being installed. It has been divided into three parts. The north and south ends are to be used as sun parlors for those patients who cannot do any kind of work. The center room will be used

Fig. 71. The piggery at the New York City Farm Colony.

During the latter months of 1914, the Department of Public Charities completed the erection of modern buildings and pens at the farm colony for the raising of hogs. Heretofore, the department has bought its pork in the open market. The 72,199 pounds raised at the New York City Farm Colony in 1916 was sufficient to supply all of the department's institutions.

Fig. 72. Outdoor work provided as a health tonic for the homeless at the New York City Farm Colony incidentally cuts food costs in the Department of Public Charities.

Many New Yorkers do not know that the Department of Public Charities maintains a very productive farm on Staten Island. During 1916, seventy-five acres were under cultivation at this farm. Over half a hundred tons of hay and straw were harvested. The vegetables raised in its gardens helped to feed the dependents in the department's several institutions.

for industrial activities. A part of the new industrial building has been occupied by women residents. The top floor has served as a sewing room. Additional dormitory space is urgently needed. (Fig. 73.)

In the industrial division almost all kinds of work were carried on. Inmates were taught the making of baskets, bead work and wood carving. When finished, the articles were taken to the homes of women connected with the New York City Visiting Committee, where sales were held. The money thus received was turned over to the persons who made the articles. Some have saved this money and bought wheel chairs for their own use. Others have gone to the city and with it started life over again.

Fig. 73. This building of the New York City Home for the Aged and Infirm, built in 1846, has for years been used to the limit of its capacity.

It is imperative that the city's accommodations for the aged and infirm be increased by at least 2,000 capacity at the earliest date possible. During periods of industrial prosperity, when only the incapacitated enter the city's homes, these institutions are full to overflowing. When the war ends and commercial conditions change, the City of New York is certain to receive an increased burden of dependent homeless persons.

Fig. 74. The New York City Home for the Aged and Infirm was established on Blackwell's Island in 1848.

It was the fourth almshouse erected by the City of New York in the Borough of Manhattan. The first[33] was built in 1736, on the "Commons" (now City Hall Park); and the second, in 1796, on Chambers Street, opposite the site of the present City Hall. The third,[34] built in 1816, is now the oldest building at Bellevue Hospital. Since the administration of charities Commissioner Homer Folks (in 1903) the city's almshouses have been called homes for the aged and infirm. In 1916, the wards of the New York City Home for the Aged and Infirm were lighted by electricity, a sun parlor was constructed for bedridden patients, and directed occupational therapy was introduced.

One man, a hopeless cripple, saved up $500 and paid his admission to a private home in New Jersey.

Under the suggestion and direction of the New York City Visiting Committee of the State Charities Aid Association and the Fruit and Flower Guild, improvement was brought about in the planning and arrangements of the grounds of the city home, and in the decoration of the buildings, by the addition of window boxes.

The Brooklyn Home for the Aged and Infirm is divided into two departments--the lodging wards and the home proper. In the former, men and women are harbored, much as they are in the Municipal Lodging House in Manhattan, until their instances of distress have been investigated and an attempt has been made to find a better solution to their problems than admission to the home. All admissions are made through the Bureau of Social Investigations.

One newcomer during 1916 was a boatswain who had been working on a British merchant ship and sending money to his wife in America with careful regularity. His ship was captured by the Germans. During this engagement, he was injured and sent to a war hospital in Berlin. His many efforts to communi-

[33]Fig. 3, p. 28. [34]Fig. 30, p. 57.

Fig. 75. The Brooklyn Home for the Aged and Infirm was established in 1795, as the Kings County Almshouse.

It came under the jurisdiction of the Department of Public Charities in 1897 (over a century after its establishment), when Brooklyn became one of the five boroughs comprising the City of New York. It is situated in a twenty-acre park, and its three dormitories provide accommodations for about 1,400 people. It serves the Boroughs of Brooklyn and Queens. Since there is no municipal lodging house in either of these boroughs it provides quarters for the temporary shelter of homeless persons.

cate with his family were without avail. He was finally befriended by a minister and permitted to return to the United States. He arrived in New York utterly penniless, to find that his wife had been dead for several months. Because of his injury he was no longer able to work, and being homeless, was admitted to the Brooklyn City Home for the Aged and Infirm.

The principal industries of the home are carried on in a tailor shop, a shoe shop for repair work only, a sewing room for women, a bandage room and an upholstery shop. A trade school was established at the Brooklyn home in 1914 for the training of residents unable to do ordinary work.

Under the auspices of the New York Association for the Blind, two teachers have been detailed to the home for the instruction of blind residents; one for women and the other for men. During the latter part of 1915 the blind classes were transferred to the trade school and the actual teaching was conducted weekly by the blind instructors. (Fig. 77.) This arrangement afforded an opportunity for the supervision of their daily work by the trade instructor. The association for the blind has aided at times by supplying materials needed for the work when they were lacking at the institution.

Fig. 76. Universally it is age's inalienable right to sit betimes in the shade and smoke, sputter and whittle. Why not in the Department of Public Charities?

The shaded grounds of the Brooklyn Home for the Aged and Infirm invite the old people to leave their chair corners and seek the healthier out-of-doors. Band concerts are held here from time to time. These old people form reading circles closely akin to the current event classes of wealthier folk. The leader of one of these circles must cater to the tastes of all or he is quickly ejected. Neither all sports nor all politics proves acceptable to all listeners. The able-bodied among the residents are expected to perform their quota of work and for those incapable of active labor sedentary occupations are provided.

Fig. 77. Hands and wits become partial substitutes for eyesight in the occupational wards for the blind of the Department of Public Charities.

There are more than 3,200 blind persons in the City of New York. Many of these are dependent upon public charity. Some are assisted in their homes through the city's relief fund for the blind. Others are cared for in the shelters of the Department of Public Charities. Under supervision, the blind can become skilled in such occupations as basket, broom and rug-making. These blind residents of the Brooklyn Home for the Aged and Infirm are becoming proficient in these occupations. In 1916, their daily work was performed under the guidance of the home's trade instructor.

During the year, there have been concerts to which all the residents were welcomed. (Fig. 76.) Band concerts were held during the summer and late into the fall. Weekly entertainments were given by residents and by persons interested in the work of the home. Social circles have existed among the residents.

THE CARE OF THE FEEBLEMINDED AND EPILEPTIC

The Mental Clinic

APPLICATIONS for admission to public institutions for the custodial care of the feebleminded and epileptic are made through the Mental Clinic of the Department of Public Charities. The City of New York maintains under this department the New York City Children's Hospital and School for the care of these patients. (Fig. 78.) The State of New York maintains five institutions for them.[35]

At the beginning of 1916, the Mental Clinic was located at Bellevue Hospital. It was later moved to the East 26th Street Pier. In December, it was again removed to its present quarters, 57 East 125th Street, Manhattan. Prior to that date, it was called the Clinic for Atypical Children. In the latter part of the year, the clinic was placed under the supervision of the superintendent of the New York City Children's Hospital and School. In this connection, it will serve as an out-patient department to this institution.

During the year 1916, a total of 2,314 patients were examined by the physicians of the Mental Clinic. (Fig. 79.) Three hundred and forty-seven had had previous examinations made, but the remaining 1,967 were new patients. The Binet-Simon tests were given to 1,687 patients during the year. The majority of the patients examined were not admitted to either state or city institutions. Some applicants did not require institutional care and it was necessary to supervise others in their homes pending a vacancy in one of the institutions. Of the 709 subjects who were referred to institutions for custodial care, 652 or 92 per cent were admitted to the New York City Children's Hospital and School on Randall's Island. The remaining fifty-seven, or only

---

[35]The institutions maintained by the State of New York for the custodial care of the feebleminded and epileptic are as follows:

The Craig Colony for Epileptics.
Letchworth Village (for epileptics).
Rome State Custodial Asylum (for the feebleminded).
State Custodial Asylum for Feebleminded Women.
Syracuse State Institution for Feebleminded.

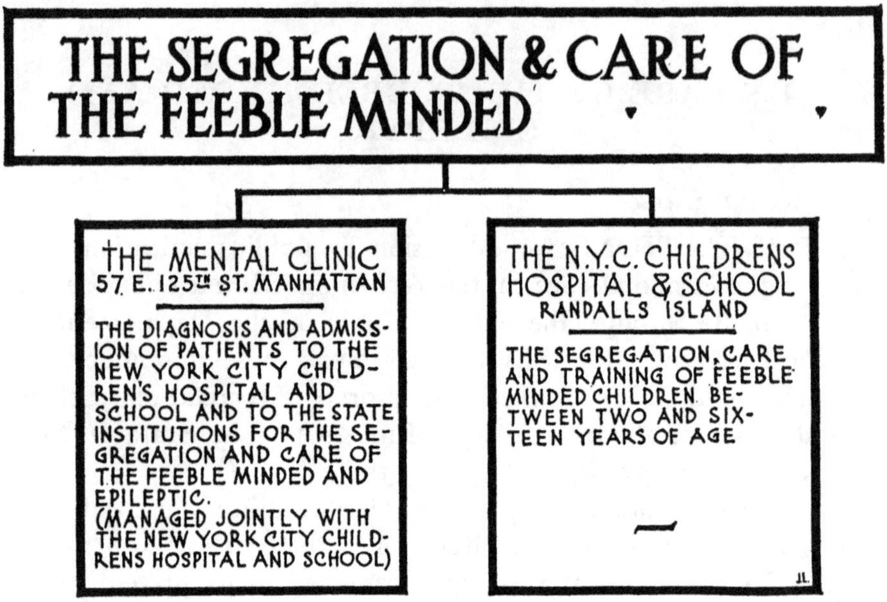

THE SEGREGATION & CARE OF THE FEEBLE MINDED

THE MENTAL CLINIC
57 E. 125TH ST. MANHATTAN

THE DIAGNOSIS AND ADMISSION OF PATIENTS TO THE NEW YORK CITY CHILDREN'S HOSPITAL AND SCHOOL AND TO THE STATE INSTITUTIONS FOR THE SEGREGATION AND CARE OF THE FEEBLE MINDED AND EPILEPTIC.
(MANAGED JOINTLY WITH THE NEW YORK CITY CHILDRENS HOSPITAL AND SCHOOL)

THE N.Y.C. CHILDRENS HOSPITAL & SCHOOL
RANDALLS ISLAND

THE SEGREGATION, CARE AND TRAINING OF FEEBLE MINDED CHILDREN BETWEEN TWO AND SIXTEEN YEARS OF AGE

Fig. 78. Organization of the activities in the Department of Public Charities for the segregation and care of the feebleminded.

Until 1868, the City of New York cared for those whom modern psychology has termed feebleminded in its almshouses or with normal children at the "Nurseries" on Randall's Island. In that year, the "Idiot Asylum" was separated from the "Nurseries" as a distinct institution. Today, the city maintains under the Department of Public Charities two activities solely for the care of the feebleminded and epileptic. The Mental Clinic examines children who are subnormal mentally, and admits them to the various public institutions maintained for their segregation and care. Through this clinic, the department plans to co-operate with the public schools and make easier the transition of pupils from their backward classes, to the school rooms of the institutions for the feebleminded. The New York City Children's Hospital and School is the only public institutions for the feebleminded in the City of New York.

8 per cent, went to one of the state institutions. Thirty-two, or 4½ per cent, of the institutional cases were transferred from their homes to the Craig Colony for Epileptics; fifteen, or 2 per cent, were transferred to Letchworth Village; six were sent to the Newark State Custodial Asylum for Feebleminded Women; and two to the Syracuse State Institution for Feebleminded Children.

The largest number of the patients sent for examination were referred by private charitable institutions. Experts on child care have urged that child-caring institutions have their charges examined whenever there is serious question as to their mental ability so that the training of the child can be adapted to its mental capacity. Four hundred and seventy-seven such uses were made of the clinic during 1916. The several bureaus and institutions of the Department of Public Charities referred 432 subjects to the clinic for examination. Other city departments referred 191. The New York Protective and Probation Association, the Society for Prevention of Cruelty to Children, and the Children's Court were agencies which made an extensive use of the services offered by the clinic. There were 510 subjects referred directly to the Mental Clinic by their relatives, friends and physicians.

Fig. 79. The detection of a mental defective at the Mental Clinic of the Department of Public Charities effects the removal of one more handicapped person from a losing struggle for survival, and forestalls the probable procreation into American social life of another lineage of incompetent and dependent Jukes.[36]

There are 33,000 feebleminded persons in New York State. Only 9,899 of these are in institutions.[37] Many of the others are at large in the City of New York. Their tendency to drift into crime, immorality, disease and poverty is shown by the blotters of the police and correction departments and the records of the courts, the hospitals and the charitable societies. Recognizing the importance of removing these potential social menaces from the community and of providing them with intelligent supervision, the Department of Public Charities has recently emphasized the development of the Mental Clinic. Here, during 1916, mental and psychological examinations were given to 3,981 persons.

There is insufficient provision made for the custodial care of the city's feebleminded and epileptic. Although the State of New York has pioneered in providing for these handicapped groups, the capacity of her institutions was taxed during 1916. The New York City Children's Hospital and School on Randall's Island was originally planned to accommodate only feebleminded and epileptic children. The Department of Public Charities believes, moreover, that this institution could render better service to its charges if its patient population were limited to feebleminded children under sixteen years of age. But owing to the limited capacity of state institu-

---

[36]Richard L. Dugdale, The Jukes, a study in crime, pauperism, diseases and heredity. E. P. Putnam. New York. 1910.

[37]Committee on Provision for the Feebleminded, State Charities Aid Association, February 1917.

tions it has been compelled to retain here patients far beyond middle age. (Fig. 81.)

The New York City Children's Hospital and School

The New York City Children's Hospital and School is on Randall's Island, opposite 121st Street, Manhattan. (Fig. 80.) For the first time in its history, it came under complete medical supervision during 1916. The administrative body was entirely reorganized. As the first radical step of this reorganiation, it was made clear to all heads of divisions that the general routine work of the institution must be always secondary to the training of the patients.

There were 1,940 patients at the hospital and school on January 1, 1916. During the year, there were 719 admissions, 496 dis-

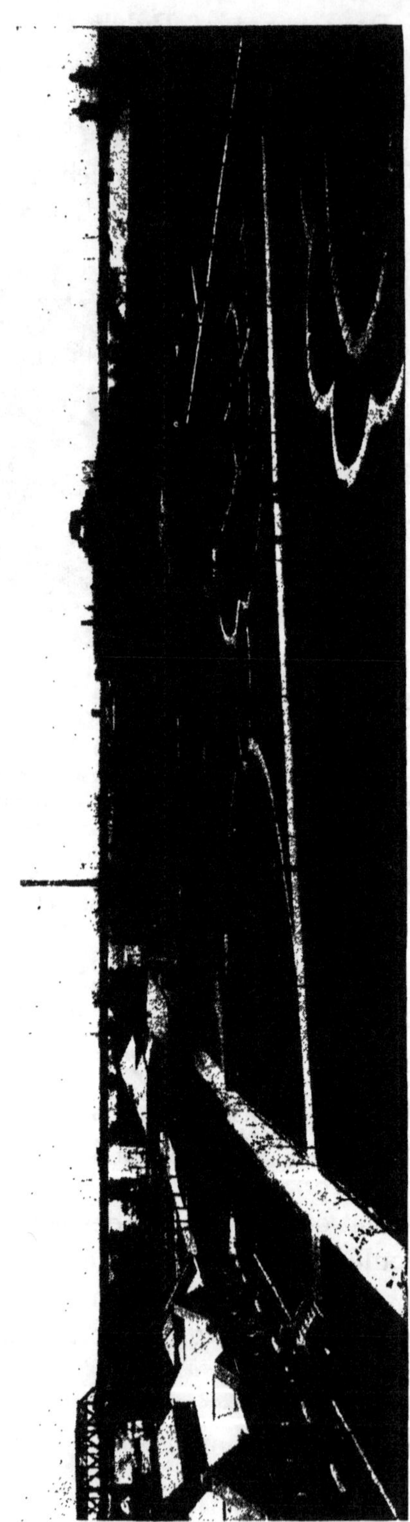

Fig. 80. The New York City Children's Hospital and School had its beginning in the "Nurseries," established by the city on Randall's Island in 1835.[38]

Its origin dates back to 1825, when the Society for the Reformation of Juvenile Delinquents erected the first "House of Refuge" in Manhattan on the present site of the Metropolitan Life Insurance Building. New York City purchased 138 acres on Randall's Island in 1835. In that year, destitute children were housed in the "Nurseries" at the north end of the island.

[38] Report of the Commissioners of the Almshouse, 1848, p. 126.

charges and 142 deaths of patients. Of those admitted, 399 were males and 320 females. More than half of them were over fifteen years of age, and about one-fourth were over twenty. About 60 per cent were received into the institution from their homes, and 38 per cent from the various city institutions. Two per cent were transferred here from state institutions for the mentally handicapped.

A medical council, composed of well known physicians, was formed during the year. The medical work was divided into six

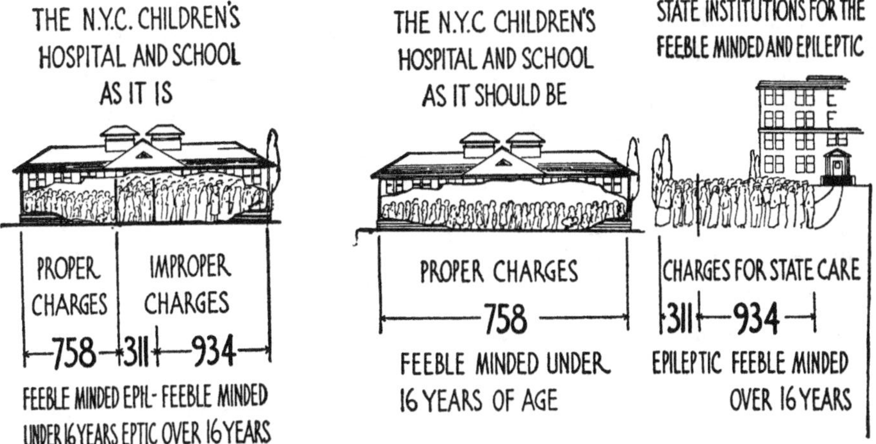

Fig. 81. Patients at the New York City Children's Hospital and School on July 1, 1916, for whom care should have been provided elsewhere.

Epilepsy and feeblemindedness are different disorders, requiring different treatments. The adult feebleminded person needs one kind of supervision and training; the child, another. Authorities agree that mental defectives should be treated according to their several distinct problems. The New York City Children's Hospital and School is designed primarily for the care and training of feebleminded children under sixteen years of age. But these make up only 38 per cent of its present patient population. An additional 47 per cent are feebleminded adults; and another 15 per cent epileptics—all of whom should be cared for in state institutions.

services, each in charge of an assistant physician. Each physician has supervision over the health and welfare of the patients in a group of buildings or cottages. He is held responsible for the maintenance of adequate records of their physical and mental state, and for their educational and industrial progress. He is expected to have an intimate knowledge of each case that he may intelligently recommend suitable training and occupation. He has charge of the discipline and supervises the housekeeping, nursing and dietary service in the cottages under his care.

Fig. 82. In these wards of the New York City Children's Hospital and School, it is demonstrated daily that medical treatment to minimize mental handicaps is preferable to imprisonment because of these handicaps.

There are 9,899 feebleminded persons in institutions in New York State.[39] Nearly one-half of these are confined in almshouses, reformatories and prisons--institutions utterly unfitted to cope with the peculiar problem presented by the feebleminded. There are 5,399 mentally defective persons in institutions designed solely for their care. The New York City Children's Hospital and School cared for 1,989 patients, during 1916.

The method of admitting new patients on only one day in the week was continued during the year. Newly admitted patients were isolated for two weeks before they were distributed throughout the hospital. In the first twenty-four hours a throat culture, as a part of a cursory physical examination, was required. A Schick test, a Wassermann test and immunization with typhoid vaccine, were also given. During the city's epidemic of infantile paralysis, not *one* case appeared on Randall's Island. The infirmary service was the lightest ever recorded. (Fig. 82.)

There has been a marked falling off in the number of contagious diseases during 1916. There were only twenty-seven cases, as compared with eighty-nine during the previous year--a decrease of 70 per cent. Eight cases of scarlet fever developed in 1915, none during 1916. There was only one case of mumps and one case of measles in 1916, as compared with forty-seven of the former and six of the latter in 1915. The most striking decline was shown in the number of diphtheria and typhoid fever patients. Of the former disease there were only two cases in 1916 as compared with sixteen in 1915. The decline in diphtheria was perhaps accomplished by the immunization of all patients who gave a positive Schick reaction. The noticeable decline in typhoid fever from thirty-two cases in 1915 to two in 1916 was undoubtedly due to the completion during the summer months of the anti-toxin vaccination of the entire population. (Fig. 83.)

There is a dental clinic in operation each morning at the New

[39]Committee on Provision for the Feebleminded, State Charities Aid Association, February, 1917.

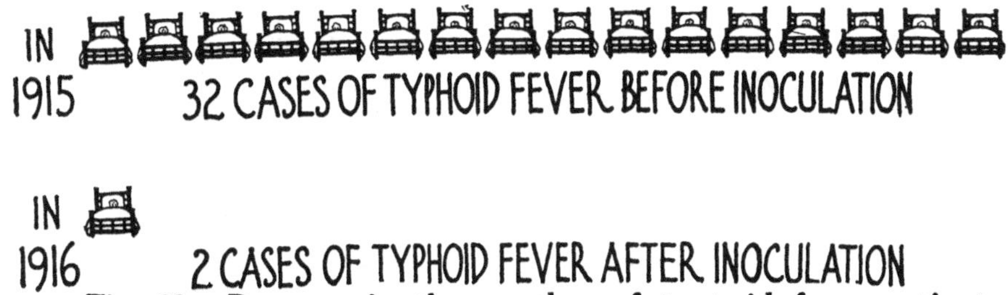

IN 1915 32 CASES OF TYPHOID FEVER BEFORE INOCULATION

IN 1916 2 CASES OF TYPHOID FEVER AFTER INOCULATION

Fig. 83. Decrease in the number of typhoid fever patients at the New York City Children's Hospital and School during the year ending December 31, 1916.

The completion of the inoculation of the entire patient population of the New York City Children's Hospital and School in 1916, resulted in a decrease of over 93 per cent in the number of typhoid fever cases at this institution during the year.

York City Children's Hospital and School. The regular use of the tooth brush is required of all patients and the teeth of each patient are examined at least once in six months.

There were eighty surgical operations performed during 1916. Eleven of these were performd on male patients, and sixty-nine on female patients. There were no deaths resulting from these operations, and in no case did the operation prove unsuccessful. (Fig. 84.) In seventy-four cases the surgical treatment was followed by a cure of the condition, and in the other six cases a marked improvement was noted. The greatest number of operations--a total of twenty--were performed for septic wounds of the hand. There were ten operations for cervical abscesses, eight for appendicitis, and five each for enlarged tonsils and inflammation of the knee joint.

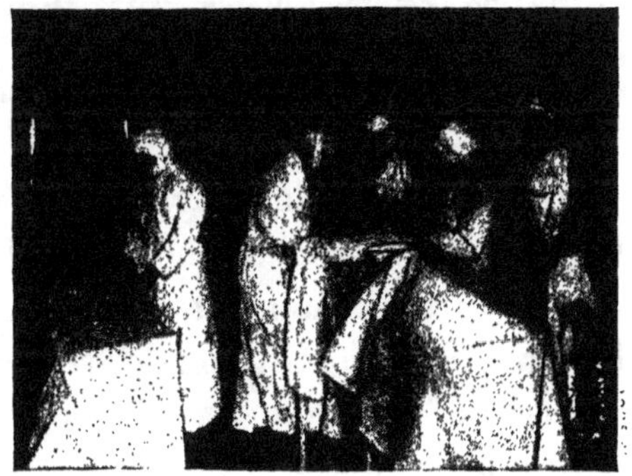

Fig. 84. The removal of an infirmity which handicaps physically the comfort and well being of an individual, already helplessly handicapped mentally, is the recurrent opportunity of modern surgery at the New York City Children's Hospital and School.

The medical service at this institution was completely reorganized during 1916. For the first time in its history, this institution came under the supervision of a medical director in March of this year. A new medical council was formed. The resident staff of physicians was almost tripled. With an infantile paralysis epidemic raging in New York City during the summer months, not one case appeared on Randall's Island. The immunizing of all patients with anti-toxin resulted in a decrease in the number of contagious diseases during the year. A complete cure resulted from seventy-four of the eighty surgical operations performed.

Matrons, or house-mothers, have been placed in charge of those cottages where no sick nursing is required. The work of supervising feebleminded and epileptic children is perhaps more difficult than that of supervising any other group. Formerly this function was performed by trained nurses, but with the hospital's budgetary allowance, it was difficult to obtain nurses qualified for this work in training and personality. To manage a cottage efficiently and yet maintain its home environment requires executive and housekeeping ability, tact, sympathy, firmness, and some knowledge of the feebleminded. It has been found desirable to establish clearly defined qualifications for these positions with a salary equal to, if not exceeding, that of the trained nurse. The gradual disappearance of ward helpers receiving from ten to fifteen dollars per month and their maintenance marks an increase in the quality of the service the institution is capable of giving to its patients. Plans are under way for the revival of the school for nurses.

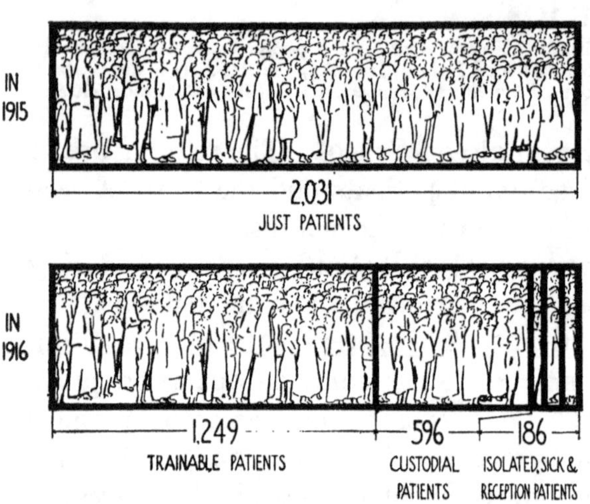

Fig. 85. Adaptability to training of 2,031 patients examined at the New York City Children's Hospital and School in October 1916.

For the first time in the history of this institution, an intelligent attempt has been made in 1916 to differentiate between the various classes of patients on Randall's Island according to their adaptability to training. Hitherto, personal appearance and physical age have largely determined a patient's opportunity for industrial and scholastic education. Now, they are classified according to their psychological ages, and an attempt is made to give them instruction commensurable with their mental ability. As a result of a survey made in October 1916, 61 per cent of the total patient population of the New York City Children's Hospital and School were adjusted to be trainable in some degree.

Before the summer of 1915 only a small percentage of the children in the institution derived benefit from the school. Twenty per cent of the 2,000 patient population was the maximum number under training at one time. Less than one hundred children at a time received industrial training; and because the work was unorganized, these monotonously performed the same tasks all day long. The opportunities of training middle and low grade patients for useful work in the institution was neglected. Scholasatic work had been emphasized as the basis of all training. Patients who were manual minded were left to deteriorate. No recognition had been given to single trait developments. Each teacher was responsible for all of the scholastic work of from fifty to eighty pupils and there was no one directly in charge of the educational work as a whole. The courses were planned after the regular curriculum of the New York Public Schools with slight regard for the peculiar mental needs of the feebleminded. The children had previously been grouped for training according to physical appearance and chronological age. Under this system of classification and training, only the exceptional child progressed.

Fig. 86. Many children with retarded mentalities respond to manual training at the New York City Children's Hospital and School and become partially, if not wholly, self supporting.

Formerly, the classes of the school were formed according to the physical appearance or chronological age of the patient. Teachers struggled to teach reading, writing and arithmetic to patients incapable of entering a kindergarten class. During 1916, a psychological survey of all patients was made the basis of an intelligent classification for training. New classes were formed. Training through the powers of touch and observation now leads up to the kindergarten classes. Transition classes bridge the difficult gap to scholastic training. For the high grade feebleminded, additional training in music and the crafts is provided.

As a basis for the reorganization of the educational system of the New York City Children's Hospital and School, a general survey was made in October, 1916. Patients were classified according to their adjudged psychological ages. It was found that 63 per cent of the 2,031 children included in the survey were trainable in some degree. (Fig. 85.) Forty-eight per cent were diagnosed as requiring custodial care. Fifty-four patients were suffering from disabilities which made necessary their isolation, from the other patients.

A supervisor was placed in charge of the newly formed edu-

Fig. 87. The practicability of training mentally deficient children in manual occupations is not a question of theory. It is demonstrated daily at the New York City Children's Hospital and School.

In the workshops of the School, carpentry, rug making, furniture repairing, basket making, and shoe repairing, all provide profitable training for the manual minded. The girls in the needlework classes are taught to make their own clothing.

cational division. This division was closely coördinated with the medical division. Physicians were consulted by teachers regarding the quantity of work to be assigned individual patients. Each pupil's medical, psychological and work record was made available to all staff members interested in his service. Weekly teachers' meetings were held for the discussion of educational problems. A system of reporting was inaugurated for keeping in touch with methods employed in training children in other institutions in the city. Instruction in Seguin training was given to

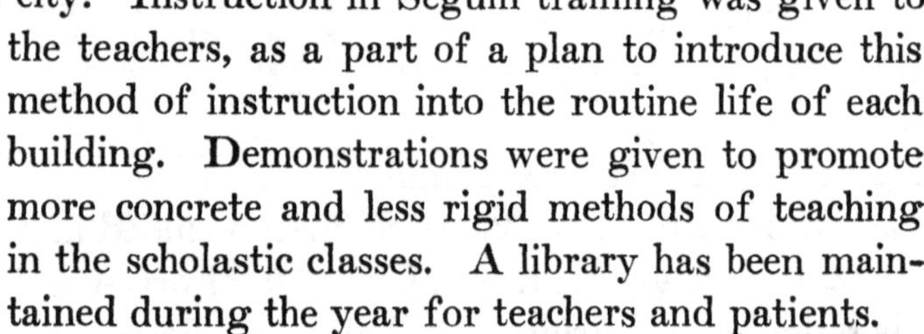

the teachers, as a part of a plan to introduce this method of instruction into the routine life of each building. Demonstrations were given to promote more concrete and less rigid methods of teaching in the scholastic classes. A library has been maintained during the year for teachers and patients.

The courses of instruction were re-planned. Cultural, industrial and recreational subdivisions were created. Ten scholastic classes were organized for children capable of advancement. Children, who after a reasonable time were unable to profit by this training, were given other work. (Fig. 86.) For the high grade feebleminded, music classes were conducted. Training was given in ensemble playing to boys who were qualified to enter the school band and to girls who were able to play orchestral instruments.

Many feebleminded and epileptic children who are not apt book scholars become proficient in the manual arts. Courses in sewing, carpentry, rug weaving, basket making and shoe repairing are among those given for these. (Fig. 87.)

Particular success has been obtained in the instruction of domestic science. Feebleminded girls take interest in cookery, cleaning, laundering, table-service and housekeeping. (Fig. 88.) This practical training enabled a number of patients, who were formerly unemployed, to accept self-supporting positions outside the institution. A similar opportunity was offered to high grade feebleminded girls adept at garment making. For high grade feebleminded boys, instruction in agriculture was offered.

The recreational activities of the hospital and school were placed under the supervision of the educational di-

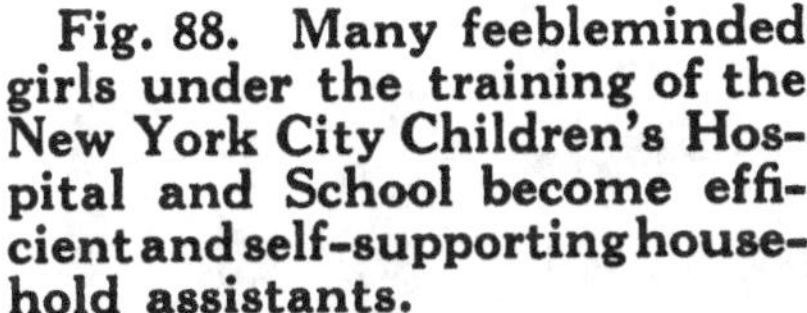

Fig. 88. Many feebleminded girls under the training of the New York City Children's Hospital and School become efficient and self-supporting household assistants.

High grade feebleminded girls respond quickly to training in domestic science. They make capable laundresses, cooks and waitresses. These girls are placed in private homes, where they remain under the supervision of the social service department of the institution.

Fig. 89. To teach the elements of good citizenship through wholesome recreation is an important part of the educational plan at the New York City Children's Hospital and School.

The importance of recreation in the education of both normal and subnormal children is no longer disputed. The Department of Public Charities provides trained workers to conduct the dancing, corrective gymnastics and games of the patients at the New York City Children's Hospital and School. Story hours, dances, band concerts, amateur theatricals and motion picture plays are among the activities provided for the feebleminded and epileptic at this institution.

vision. Two trained workers were placed in charge of the classes in physical training. (Fig. 89.) In these, calisthenics, corrective gymnastics, dancing and organized games were taught.

THE CARE AND BURIAL OF THE CITY'S DEAD

The Mortuary

THE circumstances surrounding the death of 14,180 persons in the City of New York in 1916 made it necessary for the Department of Public Charities to care for their bodies at the Mortuary. (Fig. 90.) These persons represented various nationalities, races, ages and religions. There were the bodies of men, women and children. Because unknown or unclaimed, because of unexplained circumstances connected with the cause of their death, or because of their poverty, they were attributed the city's dead.

For their care, a modern mortuary building, centrally located, has been under operation during the year. (Fig. 91.) A general renovation of the building has been under way and the routine work of the plant has been systematized. The energies of the mortuary personnel have been directed towards the reverent care and burial of the dead. Giving comfort, aid and counsel to the bereaved has been a distinct feature of the work.

People from every walk of life are brought annually to the Mortuary. The millionaire or the pauper who suddenly falls dead on the sidewalk, in a street car, in a theatre or public building, with no information upon his person by which he can be identified, and with no friend near who recognizes him, is brought here to be later removed by friends or interred in the city cemetery. A community catastrophe such as a large fire or a subway accident may bring into the mortuary doors, men, women and children from any of the diverse strata of society in the various districts of this great cosmopolitan city. When the cause of any death is unknown, or when homicide is a suspected cause, the Mortuary may be called upon to receive the dead body for an autopsy.

Into the care of this institution come the unfortunate who died in the many wards of the various private and public hospitals, unmourned or unclaimed by friends. Here are brought the

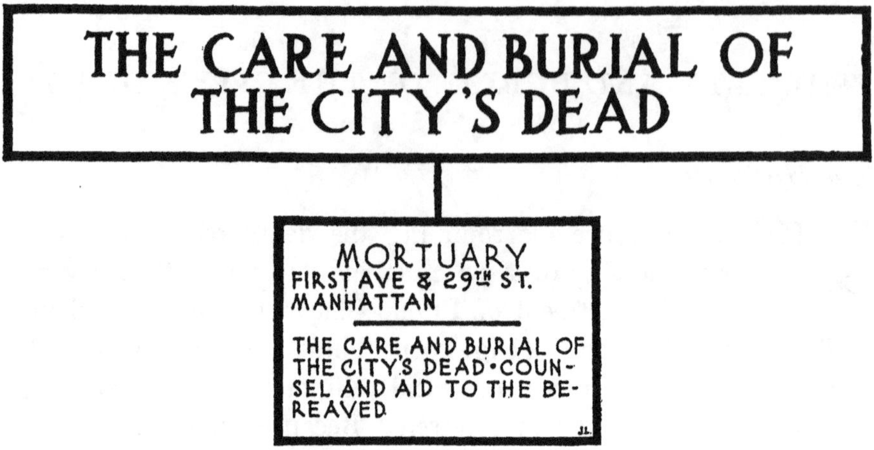

THE CARE AND BURIAL OF THE CITY'S DEAD

MORTUARY
FIRST AVE & 29TH ST.
MANHATTAN

THE CARE AND BURIAL OF THE CITY'S DEAD • COUNSEL AND AID TO THE BEREAVED

Fig. 90. The mortuary service of the City of New York underwent drastic reorganization when one central Mortuary replaced several detached morgues in various sections of the city.

It is now the policy of the Department of Public Charities to conduct a mortuary which will be at once sensitive to the dictates of humanity in the respectful disposal of the city's dead, and considerate of the welfare of the bereaved with whom it comes in contact.

uncalled for still-born from the maternity wards. Here is brought the dead leper son of a poverty stricken mother for preparation for burial. Here is received the stilled form of a stranger whose life has been taken by disease before he could complete his journey homeward. Here the remains of a father await the opportunity of a son to provide the means and make the plans for a private burial.

By January 1, 1916, the various morgues scattered through the city, together with the dark, gloomy old "morgue" at the foot of East Twenty-sixth Street were abandoned, and the new Mortuary was put into use. The new building is located at the corner of First Avenue and East Twenty-ninth Street. It is of modern, sanitary construction and provides ample capacity as a central receiving station for the city's dead.

Much attention has recently been given toward setting the institution in order. Former inefficient methods for carrying out administrative routine have been replaced by a modern system. For the first time records giving the social background of the unfortunate dead cared for at the Mortuary are being kept and made available. For the first time the correspondence of the

Mortuary is being typed and duplicate copies filed for future reference. For the first time a card index is being kept of the names and addresses of bereaved friends who call at the Mortuary to claim their dead.

The mortuary building, which had been unoccupied for some time since its erection, has needed some physical improvements. When the department moved into the building, the paint was scaling from the walls, plaster was dropping from the ceilings, pipes were leaking, and cesspools and drains were clogged. These conditions have been remedied.

Even the old "dead wagon" has been relegated to the scrap heap. Two automobile hearses with their attendants now answer calls throughout the city. (Fig. 92.) From the time that the dead body of a man, woman, or child is taken under the care of the Department of Public Charities, vigilance is exercised to insure its proper keeping.

In carrying forward the program that had been outlined for the improvement of the mortuary service, important changes in the personnel of this institution have been necessary during the year. It became clearly evident that the improvements needed could not be effected under the former superintendent. Accordingly he was asked to resign and a new head was appointed. At the same time a modification of the personnel schedule was asked for, providing for a budget of $12,300 instead of the appropriation of $6,540. This new schedule was provided for in the 1917 budget.

By virtually doubling the salary roll at the Mortuary, the

Fig. 91. The Mortuary dates back to the first city morgue, established in 1866 on the grounds of the Bellevue Hospital.

It was removed to this building which in 1915 replaced the several scattered morgue buildings in various parts of the city. The gruesome old morgue at the foot of East 26th Street had been used a half-century. The Mortuary is equipped with an attractive reception room, sanitary refrigerated vaults, autopsy rooms, a chapel and two automobile hearses.

Fig. 92. Two automobile hearses with their attendants have been substituted for the "dead wagon," which prior to 1915 had been used in transporting the city's dead.

These hearses are subject to call to all parts of the city.

quality of its service has vitally improved. Kind, willing and efficient caretakers of the city's dead, who will devote themselves to this less attractive work for twelve hours a day, seven days a week, cannot be secured for $40 a month. Employees to whom the citizen of New York City desires to entrust his dead neighbor, friend, brother, mother or daughter, do not need to bargain so poorly in marketing their services. The budgetary increase for personal service marked the exit of the all too frequently alcoholic, corrupt, ignorant, disrespectful and inconsiderate attendant. His place is now filled by the sober, kind, intelligent and humane employee.

The old haphazard method of distributing unclaimed bodies for anatomical purposes has been done away with. Students and others can no longer come to the Mortuary and upon the payment of $5 or $10 be passed to the autopsy room or secure an unclaimed body for dissection.

Fig. 93. The mortuary chapel is available to the poor in the burial of their dead.

It is here that relatives and friends identify their dead. Here the department plans to hold a solemnization service in connection with the burial of all unclaimed dead.

Comforting the Bereaved

A distinct forward step has been made during the year in humanizing the Mortuary's contact with the bereaved friends of the city's dead. The former method of compelling them to identify their dead in the refrigeration rooms has been discontinued. The bodies are now properly shrouded and placed upon a carriage and taken to the mortuary chapel for identification. (Fig. 93.)

Fig. 94. Befriending the bereaved has become a distinct feature of the city's improved mortuary service.

With the appointment of a new superintendent and the reorganization of the entire staff of employees, the quality of the mortuary service has been vitally improved. The bereaved are no longer compelled to seek information from men, hardened by contact with the sordid side of life. Especial emphasis is being placed by the Department of Public Charities upon the social service activities at the Mortuary.

No longer are persons whom death has deprived of a friend or a relative compelled to seek information from men who have been hardened by contact with the sordid side of life. They are now attended by women. (Fig. 94.) There are three women on the mortuary staff. Their function is to comfort the bereaved, to aid them in arranging for the final disposal of their dead and to protect them from unscrupulous undertakers. When a home threatens to be broken by the death of one of its members, they attempt to lend aid and counsel in its rehabilitation.

TOWARD THE OUNCE OF PREVENTION

Preventive Measures

THE Department of Public Charities has been aware that it can lend valuable aid in the alleviation of distress in New York City by giving attention to means by which it can prevent as well as relieve the miseries of the city's poor. It has realized that this is perhaps the most efficient and most economical method of alleviation.

To this end, it has attempted to make its relief constructive and preventive, as well as remedial. It has attempted increasingly to help its dependent charges to help thmselves. The humanizing activities in its various institutions and bureaus have been the chief instruments for transforming this self-help policy into action. As it comes into direct contact with the poor in their homes, it attempts to rehabilitate families, rather than to relieve the distress of individual members. It is attempting to see that the institutions which annually care for its parentless wards give training and care to these children which will fit them for self-supporting citizenship in after-life. It is attempting to give as many of these children as possible the benefit of having been reared by a real mother. (Fig. 29.) In its hospital social service work, by minimizing the dangers of relapse following hospital treatment, it transforms into action the conviction that prevention of disease is more economical, financially and socially, than its alleviation.

The Department of Public Charities has given particular attention to the rehabilitation of homeless persons who apply annually at the Municipal Lodging House for food and shelter. There are at this institution two social workers and one employment secretary, who give their full time in assisting destitute men and women to reach the first rungs of the ladder leading to self-support. As a part of this institution's policy of helping its lodgers to help themselves, persons with jobs and without money are accommodated temporarily at the Municipal Lodging House, pending the receipt of their first salary. They are then given the opportunity of reimbursing the city for this service. During the last six months of the year, 209 persons were constructively aided under this plan.

The Municipal Lodging House contributes materially toward the prevention of the spreading of communicable diseases. (Figs. 68 and 69.) Every person accommodated at the lodging house receives a physical examination. People suffering with contagious diseases are isolated. The department now exercises statutory means for requiring persons suffering with tuberculosis to receive the hospital treatment which they need.

The Department of Public Charities recognizes the need for facts regarding the social causation of poverty and distress as a basis for intelligent action in their alleviation. It has, therefore, attempted to build up a reporting system for collecting information regarding the nature of its problem as a whole and its countless number of problems within problems. It hopes through the analysis of aggregates of these facts and through the study of their causal relations to gain more intelligence as a basis for modifying its policies and endeavors so that it will increasingly contribute toward the prevention of distress. It has made beginnings in this direction in its bureaus and at various of its institutions. The Bureau of Social Investigations has given no little time to the accumulation of such records. At the various hospitals, facts throwing light upon the nature and causes of disease are being accumulated. At the Municipal Lodging House facts are being collected which will throw light upon the nature of the problem of homelessness, and which will contribute towards the meagre store of general knowledge regarding the problem of unemployment and industrial relations. For this purpose, a somewhat comprehensive survey was recently made of the natures of the ills attending the needs of some 2,000 men who applied at the Municipal Lodging House for shelter.[31]

The Department of Public Charities is attempting to prevent the propagation of feebleminded children by segregating in the city and various state institutions women of child-bearing age and men who are likely to transmit weak mental traits to their offspring. Under custodial supervision, these incapable feebleminded individuals are given education and training which often makes it possible for them to return to the world and under supervision to be productive citizens.

Not the least important contribution made by the Department of Public Charities towards the general store of knowledge aimed at the prevention rather than relief of distress is the work performed at the various pathological laboratories at the different hospitals. (Fig. 95.) Perhaps the most important change in this service was made during the year when the Brooklyn Laboratory of Pathology was established. This laboratory, formerly connected with the Kings County Hospital, is now serving the various smaller hospitals in Brooklyn, giving to these institutions fairly modern facilities for research in various fields of medicine. As a means for making available various findings of the many able physicians engaged in research and experimentation at the various departmental institutions, the department issued the first number in October, 1916, of the Hospital Bulletin of the Department of Public Charities.

Fig. 95. Research for the causes and preventatives of disease is an important part of the work of the hospitals of the Department of Public Charities.

The opportunity for scientific research in the Department of Public Charities is practically unlimited. Its employees come into direct contact with all kinds of human maladies. The department maintains five separate pathological laboratories. The year 1916 marked the organization of the Brooklyn Pathological Laboratories. In October of this year, the department began the publication of a quarterly hospital bulletin, by means of which it will give to the medical profession the data derived from its research. Here is shown the pathological laboratory of Kings County Hospital before it was merged into the Brooklyn Pathological Laboratories.

III. MODERNIZING THE MACHINERIES OF PUBLIC PHILANTHROPY

ENTRALIZATION is the Keynote of Modern Business Management - - - Concentration is Everywhere Effecting Unprecedented Economies in Time, Effort and Materials - - - In the Management of a Public Enterprise, But One Concern is Paramount to This Generation's Demand for Efficiency and Economy - - and That is Social Welfare--the End of Public Endeavor - - -

Benjamin W. Levitan, Architect

Fig. 96. The new central storehouse of the Department of Public Charities is being built on Blackwell's Island alongside the Queensboro Bridge.

This modern nine-story building, for the construction of which the Department of Public Charities secured on December 17, 1915, an appropriation of over $366,000, will serve in lieu of the now scattered storehouses of the department. In addition, it will house a modern bakery, the general drug store and a cold storage plant. The roof of the structure will be connected with the Queensboro Bridge and large elevators will make the bridge directly accessible to the island. This short route will materially cut the time and cost of transportation to the Blackwell's Island institutions. It will greatly benefit the ambulance, passenger and freight service. It will afford the hitherto isolated island institutions the protection of the Fire Department. It will give the city's best physicians ease of access to the island hospitals. Its completion will enable the Department of Public Charities to dispose of all but two of its six steamboats and to relinquish six large piers to the Department of Docks and Ferries.

III. MODERNIZING THE MACHINERIES OF PUBLIC PHILANTHROPY

THE PURCHASE AND DISTRIBUTION OF SUPPLIES

The Function of the Central Bureaus and Offices

IN maintaining an organization to befriend thousands of individuals annually, a somewhat comprehensive organic structure is necessary to keep in working order its facilities for their care. (Fig. 2.) The central bureaus and offices of the Department of Public Charities perform this function. They supplement and coördinate the work of the various institutions and bureaus which deal first hand with the destitute, the dependent, the defective and the neglected. As a part of its program for perfecting the city's service to its needy, the Department of Public Charities has made a conscious effort during 1916 to improve the efficiency of these bureaus and offices, and to make needed improvements in the equipment which it places at their disposal. It has attempted to make these improvements as economically as possible. It has endeavored to make more humane the machinery through which it necessarily performs its function in the city government.

Toward Efficiency and Economy

Reorganization in the methods of purchasing and handling supplies has been under way during the year. The department has operated a system of stores control to assist in the approval of requisitions, the making of the budget and the determination of administrative policies. The handling of supplies has been thus better organized; more adequate records have been available; requisitions have been more easily investigated; supplies have been standardized; and storehouse maxima and minima have been established. There has been inaugurated a system of distribution to the institutions of the moneys appropriated to the department for the purchase of materials, equipment and supplies.

Fig. 97. Activities in the Department of Public Charities which cut its cost of maintenance.

The Department of Public Charities produces many of the commodities used in maintaining its sixteen institutions. During 1916, the bakery on Blackwell's Island supplied eight institutions with bread.* The General Drug Department now supplies drugs to three municipal departments in addition to the Department of Public Charities. The central sewing room will eventually manufacture all of the garments and materials heretofore made in the detached sewing rooms of departmental institutions, or purchased in the open market. The departmental storekeeper estimates that the sewing room has effected a saving of approximately $1,000 by the manufacture of 36,000 articles since its establishment in 1916. The condemnation of worn out equipment, an activity begun in the latter months of 1916, has already proven itself to be an effective means of checking waste.

A system of condemnation of worn-out equipment has been established. (Fig. 97.) This provides that no new current article can be secured from the departmental storehouse without the return or accounting for of the article to be replaced.

In 1916, all of the department's sewing rooms were centralized in the shop of the old bureau of mechanics at the New York City Home for the Aged and Infirm. The room was equipped with power machines, an electric cutter, cutting tables and storage space. (Fig. 97.) One tailor, one clerk and thirty helpers were employed. During its first year of operation, this new activity produced over 36,000 articles.

During 1916, a food waste system was inaugurated, which provides for the weighing of various articles of residue food after

[40]The Brooklyn institutions of the Department of Public Charities are supplied with bread from the bakery of the Kings County Hospital. The Sea View Farms has its own bakery.

each meal. This resulted in marked savings at certain of the department's institutions. The year marked the completion of tables for the distribution of food on the per capita basis. For

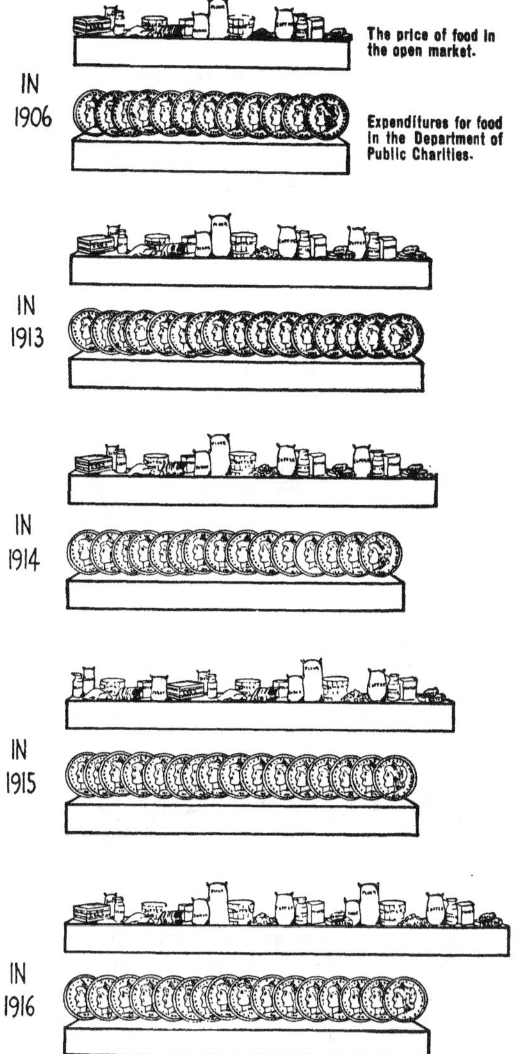

Fig. 98. The Department of Public Charities clipped over $134,000 off its food costs in 1916.[41]

Assuming that the rise in vendors' unit contract prices on eighteen principal food commodities (which represent four-fifths of the foods served on the department's institutional menus) is an accurate index of the fluctuation in price of all foods used in the Department of Public Charities, the actual departmental expenditures for food in 1916 were $134,328.78 less than they would have been had actual expenditures for food kept pace with the upward tendency of prices. While the price on these eighteen commodities was going up 14.4 per cent in1916 over 1915, the actual expenditures for all food supplies in the department went up only 2.8 per cent. During the last ten years, the former has risen 59.6 per cent, while the latter has risen only 31. per cent. Nor has the department's dinner pail been unduly stinted! Much of this saving has been due to increased activity in the elimination of food wastes.

[41]COMPARISON BETWEEN THE AVERAGE DAILY COST OF FEEDING THE EMPLOYEES AND DEPENDENTS IN INSTITUTIONS OF THE DEPARTMENT OF PUBLIC CHARITIES DURING THE YEARS ENDING DECEMBER 31, 1906 AND 1913–1916, INCLUSIVE, AND THE RISE IN UNIT COST OF 18 FOOD COMMODITIES USED BY THE DEPARTMENT DURING THESE YEARS.

Source: Statements of the Auditor in annual reports of the Department of Public Charities for the respective years.				Source: Annual Reports of the Department of Public Charities for the year ending December 31, 1916; Addenda, Financial Statements, Food Costs, Table 1.		
Year	Average daily feeding census (actual)	Total expended for food supplies (actual)	Average daily per capita food cost (actual)	Average daily feeding census (assumed)	Total cost of feeding 16,600 employees and dependents on eighteen food items at the average unit contract price of New York City vendors	Average daily per capita cost of feeding assumed census eighteen food commodities
1906	10,217	$627,079.47	16.8c	16,600	$689,493.25	11.4c
1913	14,149	1,104,175.85	21.4	16,600	962,848.50	15.9
1914	16,117	1,198,103.91	20.4	16,600	916,430.25	15.1
1915	17,466	1,358,656,06	21.3	16,600	964,933.95	15.9
1916	15,716	1,263,445.18	22.0	16,600	1,107,243.20	18.2

two years they had been in progress of compilation. These tables show the daily per capita allowance of every article of food used by the department, carried out into the quantity necessary for any given number of eaters. A marked step forward in the distribution of food supplies was made when a supervisor of foods and kitchens was assigned to the department for part time work. The full time services of an expert in this position are needed.

Feeding the Destitute

The difficulties involved in feeding the city's poor may be illustrated by showing what improvements in the menus of the

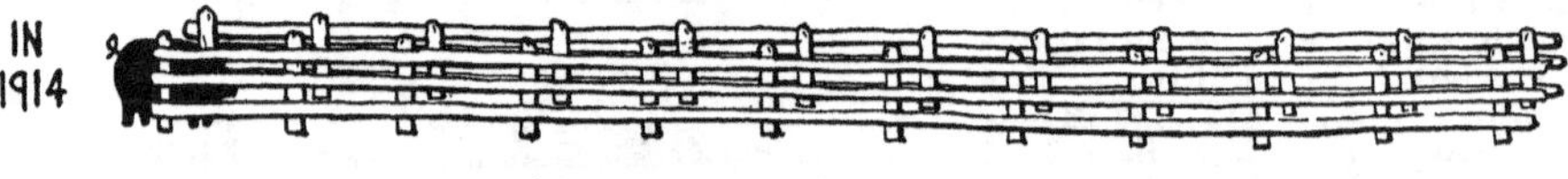

Fig. 99. Increase in pork production at the Sea View Farms (The New York City Farm Colony) from 1913 to 1916.

Until 1914, the Department of Public Charities purchased all of the pork served in its institutions. In that year, through the purchase of 400 pigs, it produced 6,128 pounds of pork at the New York City Farm Colony. In 1916, it increased this output elevenfold.

Department of Public Charities mean when translated into costs. In order to double the helping of butter given to patients in 1916, it was necessary to make other economies of over $35,000. One extra cup of coffee each day served to all the dependents of the department's institutions would cost $57,000 annually.

Soaring food prices have added materially to the cost of feeding dependents. The average price of eggs has increased from 18 cents a dozen in 1906 to 24 cents in 1915 and 29 cents in 1916. Butter has gone up from 21 cents in 1906 to 28 cents in 1915 and 29 cents in 1916. Comparing the unit costs of food supplies for 1916 with those of ten years ago, one finds that the prices paid now are 60 per cent higher than they were at that time.

In the face of these increases, the Department of Public Charities has kept its food costs down. While the price of food was going up 59 per cent in the last decade, the department has held its food costs to a rise of only 31 per cent. (Fig. 98.)

Prior to 1914, there was no pork raised at any of the department's institutions for departmental consumption. In that year, 400 pigs were purchased and a piggery was established at the New York City Farm Colony. In the first year, 6,128 lbs. of pork were raised at the farm. In 1916, this amount was increased over 1,000 per cent. (Fig. 99.) In feeding this stock, the de-

Fig. 100. Comparison of the means of transportation used in the Department of Public Charities in 1913 and in 1916.

The world's first ambulance service was established by the Department of Public Charities at Bellevue Hospital in June 1869. Then, six horse drawn vehicles answered ambulance calls forwarded by telegraph from police stations to the administrative offices of the Board of Commissioners of Public Charities and Correction. There are now 132 ambulances at the service of the City of New York, 107 of which are motor drawn. The Department of Public Charities operates twelve of these, ten of which are motor drawn.[42] The above illustration shows that this department is gradually replacing horse drawn vehicles with automobiles in all of its various activities.

partment has utilized its waste from the tables of various city institutions. Coincident with the establishment of this piggery, a coffee roasting plant was set up at the New York City Home for the Aged and infirm. (Fig. 101.)

Furnishing Drug Supplies to City Departments

The 1916 budget of the City of New York provided for the transfer of the drug departments of the Departments of Correction, Health and Bellevue and Allied Hospitals to the General Drug Department of the Department of Public Charities. This

[42]Bellevue and Allied Hospitals operate twenty-four ambulances, twenty of which are motor drawn. The Department of Health operates twenty-two ambulances, sixteen of which are motor drawn. There are seventy-four ambulances in New York City operated by private hospitals. Sixty-one of these are motor drawn. Sources: Board of Ambulance Service. The Bureau of Hospitals, The Department of Health.

Fig. 101. Since March, 1914, the Department of Public Charities has roasted in this plant all the coffee used in sixteen of its institutions.

Before the establishment of the coffee roasting plant, the Department of Public Charities bought green coffee and paid to have it roasted before delivery. In addition to serving its own institutions, the departments now roasts coffee for the Departments of Correction and Health, for Bellevue and Allied Hospitals, and for the Board of Inebriety.

transfer necessitated a complete reorganization of this activity. Pending the completion of the new central storehouse, it was removed to the East 26th Street Pier and the building formerly occupied by the morgue. (Fig. 96 and 97.)

The European war has effected the purchase of drug supplies and equipment. Steps have been taken to substitute items made in this country for those of foreign manufacture. Many materials were impossible to obtain. In a great many instances materials manufactured in this country went to fill contracts and orders from the belligerent nations. In spite of this fact, the drug department's expenditure for supplies did not exceed the sum spent in the previous year. This economy was in part made possible by the purchase of supplies at an opportune time in 1915 at much lower prices than those which prevailed during the year 1916. For example, glycerine, of which the city departments use approximately 10,000 pounds annually, was obtained in 1915 at a cost of twenty-two cents per pound. At no time since January 1, 1916, has this commodity been less than fifty-three cents per pound.

Improving Transportation in the Department

There have been several changes in the transportation facilities in the Department of Public Charities during 1916. Horse power has continued to give way to motor power. (Fig. 100.) By this change the ambulance service has been improved. The steamboat service has been curtailed. During the year, the six steamboats of the department carried a total of 2,179,060 passengers. (Fig. 102.) A total of 16,146 patients were carried to the hospitals on Blackwell's and Randall's Islands. A total of 5,741 motor trucks were carried; and 26,322 tons of supplies, handled. The bodies of 13,599 dead persons were transported to the Mortuary from island institutions and from the Mortuary to the City Cemetery on Hart's Island. During the year, the steamer "Brennan" carried 4,028 prisoners for the Department of Correction.

Fig. 102. One of the oldest of the six boats which comprise the Department of Public Charities' fleet.

Ever since 1848, when the "almshouse" was moved to Blackwell's Island, passengers have been crossing the East River in boats of the Department of Public Charities. Forty years ago, even the steam launch was unknown. Physicians often made the passage in open rowboats, through a river jammed with ice. The oldest steamer now in the service of the department, the "Fidelity," was launched in 1873. Today, there are six such steamers. Fourteen docks are maintained by the department. Records show that during 1916 these boats transported nearly 60,000 motor trucks and over 2,000,000 passengers to and from the several island institutions. The use of these boats will be modified by the installation of elevators in the new central storehouse now under construction.[43]

[43]Fig. 96, p. 106.

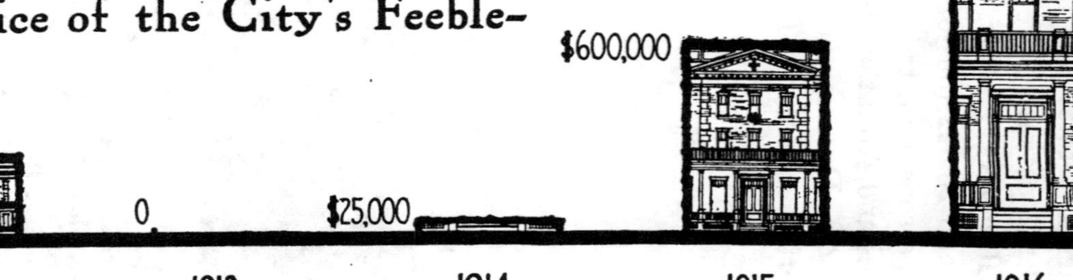

Fig. 103. Corporate stock funds authorized to improve the New York City Children's Hospital and School, 1911-1916, inclusive.[44]

In the past three years, the Department of Public Charities has been instrumental in securing the authorization of $3,724,219.50 for enlarging and altering the equipment for carrying on the various activities under its jurisdiction. Of this amount, $1,625,000 was obtained to modernize the buildings and equipment of the New York City Children's Hospital and School. There was $150,000 more obtained for this purpose in 1916 than in all of the six preceding years combined. Through these expenditures, the antiquated buildings of this institution—some of which have been standing since the days of the Civil War--will give way to a colony of cottages and administrative buildings, equipped to provide the highest standard of care to the feebleminded charges of the Department of Public Charities.

---

[44]Source: The Auditing Division. On August 31, 1911, $250,000 was issued for projects and equipment at the New York City Children's Hospital and School. Of this amount, $245,000 was rescinded and reissued on December 24, 1912.

NEW STRUCTURES AND PROJECTS

The New York City Children's Hospital and School

THE large projects in the Department of Public Charities for which funds have recently been allowed by the Board of Estimate and Apportionment include the rebuilding of the New York City Children's Hospital and School, and the Cumberland Street Hospital. Provision has also been made for erecting additional buildings at the Sea View Hospital and for modernizing the department's equipment at several of its institutions. The new central storehouse now under construction on Blackwell's Island alongside the Queensboro Bridge is of especial importance.

The City of New York recently set aside $1,600,000 for the rebuilding of the New York City Children's Hospital and School. (Fig. 103.) This sum will erect the majority of the buildings included in the department's project to reconstruct this institution on the cottage plan. (Fig. 109.) By its expenditure, brick buildings three-quarters of a century old, frame structures standing since the Civil War and remodeled cow barns will give place to modern cottages as residence quarters for patients and employees. (Figs. 110 to 112.) It will provide eight dormitory cottages and two infirmaries for patients, and two residences for the nursing and medical staffs. Many other coincident improvements will include a model kitchen plant.

The completed project calls for the erection of other dormitory cottages for both patients and employees. It calls for a reception building, in which will be housed the activities carrying forward the out-patient department of the hospital and school. It specifies the need for a central administrative building and for a recreation building, which will house a gymnasium and an auditorium.

During 1916, contracts were let for improving the lighting system on Randall's Island. Electricity is replacing gas as a means of lighting. Power is being installed for a motion picture machine. The discontinuance of the inadequate gas plant on the island will greatly improve the lighting service, lessen fire hazard and free the hospital and school from the sickening odors which have been prevalent there for years.

Other Projects in the Department of Public Charities

On December 27, 1916, the Department of Public Charities secured the appropriation of $600,000[53] to replace the present Cumberland Street Hospital. (Fig. 34.) With this expenditure, the department plans to build a seven-story building of fireproof construction, which will house complete modern hospital facilities for 300 patients under one roof. (Fig. 116.) This new structure will be located on Auburn Place between Myrtle and Park Avenues, Brooklyn. It will provide an extensive out-patient department, with over a dozen special clinical services. Besides the administrative offices, it will house separate quarters for the medical and nursing staffs for the other employees. The various classes of special patients will be segregated in separate wards. One floor will be devoted to the maternity service. Space will be provided for a school of nursing, for modern surgical rooms, for solariums and for research laboratories. Among the institution's special features will be a play room for children, an auditorium and a gymnasium.

Fig. 104. Improvement in the plant and equipment of the Cumberland Street Hospital provided by the issuance of $600,000 corporate stock on December 27, 1916.[51]

The Engineering Division of the Department of Public Charities places an evaluation of $250,000 on the present Cumberland Street Hospital building. A comparison is here made between this appraisement and the expenditures to be made for this institution's new home.[53] Since this sketch was made, the original appropriation for the new building has been increased to $800,000. The additional $200,000 was appropriated to meet the increased cost of building materials. Had this increase been taken into consideration in the preparation of this chart, the bar representing the cost of the modern structure would have been one-half inch longer than here shown.

Within the past three years, the Department of Public Charities has secured the authorization of $905,000 for additional land and buildings at the Sea View Hospital. Out of these funds have been purchased 160 acres of tillable land adjoining the hospital. Two cottages for housing old couples have been erected on the hospital grounds. Twenty-three buildings are now under construction there. (Figs. 113 to 115.) The erection of twenty-one of these will make it possible for 1,000 more patients to avail themselves of the treatment offered at this world renowned institution. Similar to the buildings now standing, they are planned to give patients an abundance of air and sunshine. A building for housing additional dispensary and recreational facilities is also being built. Another building will provide more dining room space and an auditorium for the hospital.

Fig. 105. One of the modern laundry plants in the Department of Public Charities.

The laundries of the Department of Public Charities serve sixteen institutions with an aggregate bed capacity for over 13,000 people. Eleven of these institutions are hospitals demanding piles of immaculate aseptic linen daily. Approximately 28,000 pieces of linen go through these laundries daily. The department is centralizing its laundry plants on Blackwell's Island,[46] in Brooklyn and in Richmond. The patients of the New York City Children's Hospital and School assist largely in doing the laundry work for their own institution and for the Municipal Lodging House (or for an aggregate daily registration of over 2,600 persons). The photograph shown above is of the Greenpoint Hospital laundry.

Approximately $100,000 has been spent recently for the installation of fire walls in most of the buildings occupied by patients in the different institutions of the Department of Public Charities. Hitherto, these buildings have been considered fire hazards. The work was planned and executed by an expert on fire protection, and the buildings are now in fairly safe condition.

When a children's service was established at the Coney Island Hospital in 1915, there were no facilities provided for out-door sleeping porches or airing balconies. To meet this requirement,

---

[46]On March 1, 1917, the centralization of the laundry plants on Blackwells Island was affected. Through this consolidation of the laundries of two hospitals, two training schools for nurses, and a home for the aged and infirm, two laundry buildings have been released for other purposes. The departmental superintendent of laundries estimates that this consolidation resulted in a saving of $15,000 during the first six months of operation.

Fig. 106. Blackwell's Island is spanned by the Queensboro Bridge, the second longest cantilever bridge in the world.[47]

With the opening of the new central storehouse of the Department of Public Charities, traffic to the institutions on Blackwell's Island will be directed by way of this bridge and the large elevators of the storehouse.[43] The bridge connects 59th and 60th Streets at Second Avenue, Manhattan, with Jackson Avenue at Queens Plaza, Queens. It was opened for pedestrians and vehicles on March 30, 1909.

an adequate porch, which can be enclosed in stormy weather, was constructed in the summer of 1916. Approximately $40,000 was expended during the year in the installation of screens in the institutions of the department. A $75,000 laundry is nearing completion at the Kings County Hospital. This plant will provide laundry facilities for all of the institutions in Brooklyn. (Fig. 105.)

The New Central Storehouse

On December 17, 1915, the Board of Estimate and Apportionment authorized the expenditure of $366,123 for the erection of a central storehouse and service building on Blackwell's Island alongside the Queensboro Bridge. (Figs. 96, 106 and 107.) This building will largely solve the physical problem of handling, storing and distributing supplies for the institutions of the Department of Public Charities in the different boroughs of the city. It will provide a direct route to the institutions on Blackwell's Island. It will be an efficient substitute for the scattered storehouses of the department.

One floor of the new storehouse will be occupied by a modern bakery, equipped to supply bread to all public institutions in the

---

[47] Figs. 106 and 107 present a panoramic view of the central section of Blackwell's Island.

Fig. 107. The City of New York purchased Blackwell's Island in 1828—one hundred and ninety-one years after the Indian name of the island, "Minnahanonck," had been changed by the Dutch to "Varken" or "Hog Island."[47]

It was purchased for $32,000 from Robert Blackwell whose homestead, built a century and a half ago, is still standing. The New York County Penitentiary was established in 1832; the Smallpox Hospital, in 1837; the Almshouse, in 1846; and the Blackwell's Island Hospital (comprising a lunatic asylum and wards for the treatment of children and convicts), in 1847. There are now on Blackwell's Island two prisons, three hospitals, two nurses' homes and one home for the aged.

city. (The bakery which it will replace is partially underground and would not be tolerated by the city if operated by a private concern.) Another floor will house the general drug store, and a plant for manufacturing drugs and surgical supplies for all of the city departments and institutions. One floor will be used for cold storage, and others for dry and sanitary storage. The roof or concourse of this nine-story building will be connected with the Queensboro Bridge by two short cantilever bridges--one for incoming, and another for outgoing vehicles. Large elevators will lift these conveyances from the island to the bridge.

Commissioner Adamson, of the Fire Department, has pronounced the institutions on Blackwell's Island "one of the greatest potential fire hazards in the city." The comparative ease of access made possible by these elevators will largely eliminate this hazard by giving these institutions the direct protection of the Fire Department. They will, moreover, provide for the swift transportation of passengers and freight. Patients, now transferred four times in transit to the island hospitals, will be delivered by ambulances to the doors of these institutions without delay and without the agonies of transfer. These hospitals will become directly accessible to the city's best physicians and surgeons, and to the thousands of patients and friends of patients who visit them annually. Besides the economies which will naturally result from these improved transportation facilities, the Departments of Public Charities and Correction will be enabled to dispose of most of their fleet of steamboats, and several large docks will then be transferred to the Department of Docks and Ferries.

IV. FOR TOMORROW

EXCERPTS FROM THE PROGRAM OF THE DEPARTMENT OF PUBLIC CHARITIES

HE Wastes of the Present War are Forcing Commonwealths to Their Wits' Ends in Devising Means of Saving Men for Society . .
New Estimates are Being Placed Upon the Individual .

¶ Charitable Institutions, Formerly Refuges for Discarded Dependents, are Becoming Foundations for the Discovery of Dormant Talents .

¶ Philanthropy more than ever before is Challenged to Prevent the Catastrophe of a Useless and Dependent Individual . .

Fig. 108. The Blackwell's Island Reef Light.

Through half a century of stormy and starlit nights, this solitary sentinel, tended by the Department of Public Charities, has welcomed into the shelter of New York City's lower anchorages, skippers and crafts from wherenot--guiding them through the hidden rocks and swift tidal currents which imperil the narrow channel of the East River, as it rounds Hallets Point at Hell Gate and divides itself across the upper nose of Blackwell's Island.

IV. FOR TOMORROW

In the Department of Public Charities

EXCERPTS FROM THE PROGRAM OF THE DEPARTMENT OF PUBLIC CHARITIES

General Policies

TOMORROW'S program for the Department of Public Charities aims to extend the activities reported upon in the foregoing pages. It does more. It aims to supplement these with such other activities as will be demanded by the development of all of this department's resources for helpfulness. The Department of Public Charities confronts a fourfold challenge. (1) It should see that the thousands of dependents coming directly and indirectly under its care are adequately provided with such basic necessities of a normal life as food, shelter and clothing. (2) It should aid in bringing these charges to a state of self-dependency by helping them to secure such other necessities of a normal life as will counteract their social retardation--whether it be caused by poverty, unemployment, lack of training, sickness, physical or nervous disability, inferior mentality, orphanhood, homelessness, destitution or neglect. (3) Through measures of prevention, it should aim to assist persons near poverty's border line to avoid dependency and to establish their descendants in a state of social and economic security. (4) It should, moreover, keep the machineries necessary for the efficient and economical performance of these functions ever sensitive to those humane and benign motives which have called them into being.

In Adjusting the Maladjusted

The Department of Public Charities should continue to develop its resources for extending non-institutional relief to the needy of the City of New York. It should continue the policy of treating distress from the standpoint of the family unit rather than of the individual unit; by helping applicants not as individuals but as members of family groups. It should continue to insist that the highest standards of institutional care prevail in all charitable institutions, public and private, receiving city charges. It should develop an intelligent and humane system of caring for the city's foundling children in good homes rather than in institutions. It should continue the centralization of its non-

Donn Barber, Architect

Fig. 109. Looking into the future, the Department of Public Charities has dreamed of a New York City Children's Hospital and School that is to be.

The Department of Public Charities recently secured the authorization by the Board of Estimate and Apportionment of $1,000,000 for the construction, alteration and equipment of buildings at the New York City Children's Hospital and School. This appropriation will make it possible in the near future to rehouse the entire patient population at this institution. The completed project, embodying a model community of cottages beautified by gardens, will place this institution's physical outlay among the finest of its kind in the world.

institutional relief activities. It should increasingly co-operate with other city departments in eliminating useless duplication of effort in providing for the needy, and in protecting the citizens' charity fund from misuse.

In the Care of the Sick

All persons aided by the Department of Public Charities, including those supported in private institutions by public moneys, should receive adequate medical and surgical service. Periodical examinations should be made to ascertain whether dependents need these services. The methods of treatment in the care, cure and prevention of sickness through the department's eleven hospitals and thirty odd clinics should be raised to the highest possible standard. The usefulness of these stations as community health centers, co-operating with the Department of Health and Bellevue and Allied Hospitals in the advocacy of such contagious health measures as sanitation, fresh air, good food and recreation, should be developed. The results of their experiences and researches, as additions to the general store of medical knowledge, should know no territorial boundary.

In the Care of the Homeless

Homelessness, like many other causal conditions of poverty, results from a complexity of causes within individuals and attendant upon certain social usages over which the Department of Public Charities can have no direct control. It is in a position, however, to provide affirmation to the need of such recognized measures as the organization of the employment market; the regularization of industry; the provision of social insurance; and such other steps of control over the circumstances surrounding the birth, education and training of children as will prevent the adults of succeeding generations from throwing themselves or being thrown, dependent and homeless, upon the public thoroughfares. That the department should increasingly do. Its immediate end, however, is to provide comfortable shelters for the homeless, where they may be, so far as possible, self-supporting. It should encourage also such intelligent and humane treatment of individual homeless men and women as will effect the rescue from dependency of a maximum number of them.

In the Care and Segregation of the Feebleminded

The authorization in 1916 by the Board of Estimate and Apportionment to expend $1,000,000 for the construction, alteration and equipment of buildings at the New York City Children's Hospital and School will make it possible in the near future to

Donn Barber, Architect

Fig. 110. Eight of these modernly equipped cottages will house the high grade feebleminded patients at the New York City Children's Hospital and School.

Each building will have two floors, equipped as special units and providing separate quarters for the various classes of patients. Each cottage will have two dormitories, a school room, a manual training shop, a recreation room and a dining room seating 120 patients. They will be of fireproof construction, and finished with sanitary flooring. Heated conveyances will transport food to these cottages from the main kitchen of the institution.

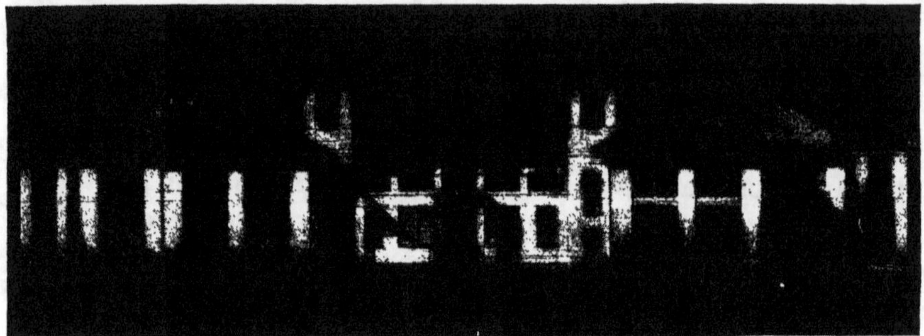

Donn Barber, Architect

Fig. 111. This proposed infirmary makes a tangible testimony to the higher standard of medical service to be given to the patients of the New York City Children's Hospital and School.

There will be two of these buildings, each two stories high and designed to accommodate 180 patients. There will be four hospital wards in each building, having a combined capacity of 140 beds. Each floor will provide a complete infirmary unit with a kitchen and pantry, an isolation ward, a day room and airing balconies. Glass enclosures on the south side of the day rooms will enable the patients to live in the fresh air and sunlight in the daytime.

rehouse the entire patient population of this institution. The completed project, embodying a model community of cottages beautified by gardens, will place this institution's physical outlay among the finest of its kind in the world. (Fig. 109.) The Department of Public Charities should plan to bring the service of the hospital and school up to the standard set in planning its physical superstructure. It should plan, moreover, to co-operate with the state authorities in removing the city's dependent feebleminded children from the social and economic competition of the normally minded. By bringing the feebleminded into an environment designed to foster their training for self-support, the

Donn Barber, Architect

Fig. 112. This dormitory will provide comfortable residence quarters for nurses at the New York City Children's Hospital and School.

It will contain twenty-five bedrooms, eight separate baths, a dining room, a kitchen and recreation quarters.

department would render an increasing service to them and to posterity--ever menaced by their potential power to produce "more pauperism, degeneracy and crime than any other one force."[48]

In the Care and Burial of the City's Dead

The Department of Public Charities should continue its policy of establishing the standard of the city's mortuary service on the highest plane of efficiency and humanity. That the city's dead be given humane care and burial and that their friends and relatives be given comfort, counsel and aid, should be the constant concern of this department.

Renwick Aspinwall and Tucker, New York
Edward F. Stevens, Boston, Associated Architects

Fig. 113. There are twenty-one of these pavilion buildings under construction at Sea View Hospital.[49]

They will add 1,000 beds to the present capacity of the sanatorium. Each will contain four wards, accommodating forty-eight patients. A group of thirteen will be devoted to men, the remaining eight to women.

Efficient and Economical Management Should be Perfected

Business sagacity should continue to pervade the management of the Department of Public Charities. The systems of control over the department's supplies, equipment and food commodities should be perfected. The food waste system, which has resulted in decreasing the department's food costs, should be developed. The centralization of the heat, light and power plants at various of the department's institutions, and of such activities as laundries and sewing rooms, should result in increased economies. The General Drug Department should be reorganized to facilitate in the purchase and distribution of supplies. The budget system should be perfected and extended to the institutions and bureaus of the department.

---

[48]Amos W. Butler, The Burden of Feeblemindedness; Proceedings of the National Conference of Charities and Corrections, 1907, p. 10.

[49]Figs. 114 and 115; pp. 128, 129.

Renwick Aspinwall and Tucker, New York
Edward F. Stevens, Boston, Associated Architects

Fig. 114. This new dining hall at the Sea View Hospital[50] will be convertible into an auditorium.

Additional dining room space will be provided in this building, when the capacity of the hospital has been increased by the erection of other buildings now under construction.[49] The dining room will be convertible into an auditorium.

Needed Structures and Projects

The Department of Public Charities has been instrumental in the past three years in securing the authorization by the Board of Estimate and Apportionment of $3,724,219.50 for the building, rebuilding and equipment of the various institutions carrying forward its activities.[51] The expenditure of this money will mark important improvements at the Sea View and Cumberland Street Hospitals, the New York City Children's Hospital and School, and at practically all of the other departmental institutions. (Figs. 110 to 116.) It provided for the erection of a central storehouse and elevator which will make the Blackwell's Island institutions directly accessible to the boroughs of Manhattan and Queens. (Fig. 96.) It allowed improvements in fire protection and in water transportation. It is essential that additional accommodations be provided at the city homes for the aged at the earliest possible date. (Fig. 76.) Funds are needed for the erection of a central power plant on Blackwell's Island and for conduits to conduct the power from this plant to the various island institutions. A garbage incinerator is also needed on the island. Increased funds should be devoted to the repair of the department's buildings.

Improvements Needed in Quantity and Quality of Personal Service

All positions in institutions receiving wards of the Depart-

---

[50]Fig. 51, p. 66.

[51]For an itemized account of the projects in the Department of Public Charities for which corporate stock funds have been requested, have been allowed or will be needed, see The Annual Report of the Department of Public Charities for the year ending December 31, 1916, Addenda, Financial Statements, Corporate Stock Authorizations and Needs, Tables 1-3.

Renwick Aspinwall and Tucker, New York
Edward F. Stevens, Boston, Associated Architects

Fig. 115. The recreation facilities to be housed in this building will shorten the tedious hours of convalescent tubercular patients at Sea View Hospital.[49]

Employment and recreation under medical supervision have definite therapeutic value in the treatment of tuberculosis. These are the hospital's means of strengthening the patient's power of resistance before discharging him into his former environment. Space for such activities will be provided in this new building. It will also house a dispensary.

ment of Public Charities should be adequately manned and salaried. Institutions can then have no excuse for carrying forward any of their activities by sacrificing the welfare of dependents whom they exist to serve. Increased appropriations for personal service are neded at the department's institutions. Regardless of the fact that appropriations for this purpose were higher in 1916 than at any time heretofore, it has been necessary in some instances to maintain the institutions by the labor of dependents when such measures might justly occasion criticism. The city's failure in such instances to subordinate the maintenance of its institutions to the welfare of its charges is hardly excusable because unconscious rather than designed.

Activities Needed to Prevent Distress

A bureau of social research is needed in the Department of Public Charities.[52] Under the direction of this bureau, the department would utilize the abundance of social and medical data available at its sources of contact with its dependents. By standardizing the present systems employed at the various institutions and bureaus in reporting these facts, this material would be given a value it has not hitherto possessed. As a permanent census bureau, conducting special investigations, this new division would provide a basis of information which would increasingly enable the department to attack distress at its origins.

The Department of Public Charities should continually widen its field of helpfulness to its dependents after they have left the

[52]The organization of this bureau was begun in June, 1917, when the services of I. M. Rubinow, Ph. D., were secured as its director.

Ludlow and Peabody, Architects

Fig. 116. A distinct forerunner of the future in hospital construction, the new Cumberland Street Hospital will be a formidable ally to the cause of health in the Borough of Brooklyn.

It will house a complete hospital plant under one roof. Each ward will have a capacity for twenty-four beds and will be divided into six cubicles by half glass partitions. This will permit an unobstructed view of the entire ward, yet will afford greater privacy and alow a stricter classification of patients. A special tonsil ward, adjacent to the out-patient department, will provide space for the overnight retention of patients. The space planned for living quarters for the nurses and staff can be used for patients, if later demands upon the institution require increased ward capacity. The building will cost $800,000.[53] It will be fireproof throughout.

doors of its institutions and bureaus. Its aim should be to re-establish the dependent in normal life. Follow-up and after-care systems should insure the provision of adequate measures in individual cases against the recurrence of conditions which have required the services of this department.

A Department of Public Welfare Needed

The Department of Public Charities recognizes the desirability of consolidating all public humanitarian work in the City of New York into a department of public welfare. Such a department should concern itself with securing efficient and effective co-operation between the large philanthropic forces and the more intimate community resources aimed at the betterment of the general social and living conditions in the City of New York.

---

[53]The original appropriation on December 27, 1916, called for an expenditure of $600,000 for the construction and equipment of the new Cumberland Street Hospital. In 1917, it was necessary to increase this acount to $800,000 because of the soaring prices of building materials. The original plan of erecting the new hospital on the site of the old was abandoned. The new building is being erected upon city property, formerly used by the Department of Education for recreational purposes.

BY WAY OF CONTRAST

In Adjusting the Maladjusted

1913

The groups of field workers in the several boroughs were never gathered for the purpose of receiving uniform instruction or for general discussion.

1914

Quarterly conferences of the entire staff of field workers of the Bureau of Social Investigations made possible uniform instruction and general discussion.

1914

The relief work to the maladjusted was divided among the Bureaus of Dependent Adults and the Children's Bureaus. Duplication and waste of effort and expense was the result.

1915

The Bureau of Social Investigations was established and all types of relief to the maladjusted were combined and administered by district offices scattered throughout the city.

There was no consolidation of the information that had been obtained by the department about any one given family or individual.

A central control index was established, assembling information concerning each family or individual, and preventing duplication in record keeping.

A person in need of more than one form of relief was compelled to travel to several widely separated offices where the special services of the department were conducted.

The city was divided into eight districts with an office conveniently located in each of them for the purpose of granting necessary relief of any character within the scope of the department's work.

There were no offices of the Department of Public Charities in the Boroughs of the Bronx and Queens.

An office was established in each borough of the greater city.

Many children whose misfortune was due solely to poverty, suffering or distress were taken by their mothers to the Children's Court. There were no means of bringing them in contact with the Department of Public Charities.

A representative of the Department of Public Charities was assigned to the Children's Court, making the relief of this department immediately available to children whose misfortune was due solely to poverty.

While awaiting relief the blind were compelled to stand in long lines in the street.

The blind were gathered in an armory to receive relief and were thus served far more comfortably.

BY WAY OF CONTRAST

In Adjusting the Maladjusted

1914

Only emergent maternity cases were treated in the private hospitals at public expense.

1915

A system was established for registering maternity cases at private hospitals and for providing prenatal treatment and instruction there at public expense.

1915

The City of New York, although annually entrusting thousands of dependents to the care of institutions and agencies under private management, knew little or nothing of the service and training given by these institutions.

1916

The Department of Public Charities established the Bureau of Institutional Inspections with a trained force of inspectors to examine into the affairs and methods of training at these institutions.

There were no children boarded out in private families. All were sent to private child caring institutions.

A Children's Home Bureau was organized and 217 children were placed in private families within three months.

In the Care of the Sick

1913

Pathological laboratories of the Brooklyn hospitals were conducted at each of the smaller institutions and at the Kings County Hospital.

1916

In October, the pathological work of the four hospitals were centralized in the Brooklyn Laboratories of Pathology.

1915

There was a dual service medical board at the Central and Neurological Hospital.

1916

A unified medical board was appointed.

The Central and Neurological Hospital was administered as a division of the New York City Home for the Aged and Infirm.

It was administered as one of the institutions under the hospital system.

There was no physician on the staff of the Pelham Bay Home, a convalescent home for mothers and babies.

The services of an attending physician were secured.

BY WAY OF CONTRAST

In the Care of the Homeless

1913

In times of severe industrial depression, any overflow of applicants to the Municipal Lodging House slept in the morgue building or sought shelter in the prison pens on Twenty-sixth Street pier, where standing room only was available.

1914

By securing the Twenty-fourth Street Recreation Pier as an annex to the Municipal Lodging House, the Department of Public Charities was able to give comfortable and clean sleeping accommodations to every homeless dependent applicant.

1913

The Municipal Lodging House referred 582 men to the Magistrates' Courts as vagrants. Four hundred and thirty-nine convictions were obtained.

1916

Thirty-five lodgers were referred to courts as vagrants and in each instance a conviction was obtained.

No systematic effort was made to obtain outside paid employment for the men and women at the New York City Farm Colony.

An employment bureau was established and 317 persons were placed in outside positions.

In the Segregation and Care of the Feeble-minded and Epileptic

1915

At the New York City Children's Hospital and School, patients were classified largely according to their physical appearance and without regard to their mental capacity.

1916

A survey of all patients was made. A system of classifying patients for educational work according to psychological age was instituted.

At the New York City Children's Hospital and School there were thirty-two cases of typhoid fever.

Immunization of all patients was completed and there were only two cases of typhoid fever.

At the New York City Children's Hospital and School there were eighty-nine cases of contagious diseases.

There were twenty-seven cases of contagious diseases—a decrease of 69.6 per cent under those of the previous year.

Records of psychological examinations were not kept.

A system of keeping adequate records of all such examinations was installed.

There were two medical boards with divided responsibilities.

Responsibility was centered in one advisory medical board.

BY WAY OF CONTRAST

In the Segregation and Care of the Feeble-minded and Epileptic

1915	1916
There was one resident physician in the pay of the city.	Eight resident physicians were employed.
The institution provided dental service during only a few hours each week.	Dental service was provided on three days of each week.
There was no effective quarantine for incoming patients.	An effective quarantine for incoming patients was instituted.
In March 1916, the city was paying $160 per month for medical service at the New York City Children's Hospital and School. This service was subsidized by private philanthropy.	In November 1916, the city was paying $1,225 per month in medical salaries at this institution, and private philanthropy was no longer called upon.
Eleven buildings, constructed before 1869, were in use at the New York City Children's Hospital and School.	Allowance was made for the expenditure of $1,000,000 for the construction of new buildings and remodeling of old buildings.

In the Care and Burial of the City's Dead

1915	1916
Morgues were scattered throughout the city.	A new and sanitary mortuary was opened at First Avenue and Twenty-ninth Street, Manhattan.
A "dead wagon" was in use.	Two automobile hearses with attendants call for bodies throughout the city.
Bereaved friends and relatives were compelled to identify their dead in the refrigeration rooms of the old morgue.	The bodies are now properly shrouded and taken into the mortuary chapel for identification.
There were no women employed at the morgue to serve the seventy odd thousand people who came annually to that institution on their errands of sorrow.	Three women employees were appointed at the Mortuary.

CHRONOLOGICAL NOTES

ON THE DEVELOPMENT OF THE DEPARTMENT OF PUBLIC CHARITIES OF THE CITY OF NEW YORK

1609 Henry Hudson rounded Sandy Hook, September 2.

1623 Manhattan Island purchased from the Indians by the Dutch West India Company.

1654 A home for orphan children founded. This was used for the temporary accommodation of the indentured children of the West India Company.

1658 The first hospital on American soil established--later called "Old Hospital" or "Five Houses."

1664 The City of New York founded by the British.

1665 A Mayor and Board of Aldermen appointed by proclamation of the first English Governor, Col. Richard Nicols, July 12th.

1695 The passage by the General Assembly of an "Act to enable the City of New York to relieve the poor."

1736 The first almshouse of the City of New York established as the "Public Workhouse and House of Correction."

1795 The Brooklyn Home for the Aged and Infirm opened as the Kings County Almshouse.

1798 A board of five "Commissioners of the Almshouse" appointed.

1816 The third almshouse opened at "Belle Vue."

1835 The New York City Children's Hospital and School established as the "Nurseries" on Randall's Island.

1848 The "Almshouse" (New York City Home for the Aged and Infirm) established on Blackwell's Island.

The almshouse at "Belle Vue" became Bellevue Hospital.

1849 The Kings County Hospital separated from the Kings County Almshouse.

A board of ten "Governors of the Almshouse Department of the City of New York" appointed.

1857 The New York City Hospital established on Blackwell's Island as the "Island Hospital," December 15th.

1860 A board of "Commissioners of Pubilc Charities and Correction" appointed.

1866 The Mortuary established as the "city morgue."

1875 The City Hospital School of Nursing opened as the "Charity Hospital Training School for Nurses," October 1st.

The Metropolitan Hospital founded on Ward's Island as The "New York Homeopathic Hospital."

1892 The Metropolitan Hospital Training School for Nurses established.

1893 The Department of Public Charities and the Department of Correction organized as separate branches of the city government.

The Department of Public Charities administered by a board of three commissioners, one acting as president.

1896 The Municipal Lodging House opened.

1897 The Kings County Hospital Training School for Nurses established.

1902 The "Board of Commissioners of Public Charities" abolished and a commissioner and two deputies appointed.

The New York City Farm Colony established.

The Cumberland Street Hospital opened.

The Cumberland Street Hospital Training School for Nurses founded.

The Bradford Street Hospital established, November 25th.

The Bellevue and Allied Hospitals removed from the jurisdiction of Department of Public Charities.

1910 The Coney Island Hospital established, May 8th.

1913 The Pelham Bay Home opened as the "Hunter's Island Convalescent Home," August 19th.

The Sea View Hospital established, October 28th.

1915 The Greenpoint Hospital established, October 4th.

The Bureau of Social Investigations organized.

1916 The Central and Neurological Hospital established as a separate institution.

The Bureau of Institutional Inspections organized.

The Children's Home Bureau organized.

The Brooklyn Laboratories of Pathology opened.

The Mental Clinic established.

The reorganization of the New York City Children's Hospital and School. An appropriation of $1,000,000 secured for the construction, alteration and equipment of its buildings.

An appropriation of $600,000 secured for the construction of a hospital to replace the Cumberland Street Hospital.

Ground broken for the New Central Storehouse on Blackwell's Island.

DIRECTORY
of the
DEPARTMENT OF PUBLIC CHARITIES
of the
City of New York

OFFICIALS—GENERAL OFFICES

Commissioner, HON. JOHN A. KINGSBURY; Tenth Floor, Municipal Building, Manhattan.

First Deputy Commissioner, HON. HENRY C. WRIGHT; Tenth Floor, Municipal Building, Manhattan.

Second Deputy Commissioner, HON. WILLIAM J. DOHERTY; 327 Schermerhorn Street, Brooklyn.

Third Deputy Commissioner, HON. FLOYD W. FISKE, Tenth Floor, Municipal Building, Manhattan.

Secretary, VICTOR S. DODWORTH; Tenth Floor, Municipal Building, Manhattan.

OFFICES, BUREAUS, INSTITUTIONS AND CLINICS

AGED AND INFIRM, THE NEW YORK CITY HOME FOR THE; Blackwell's Island, Manhattan; Edward E. McMahon, *Superintendent.*

AGED AND INFIRM, (BROOKLYN DIVISION) HOME FOR THE; Clarkson Street near Albany Avenue, Brooklyn; John F. FitzGerald, M.D., *General Medical Superintendent;* Mortimer D. Jones, M.D., *Superintendent.*

ARCHITECT, DEPARTMENTAL, THE ENGINEERING DIVISION; Tenth Floor, Municipal Building, Manhattan, Sylvester A. Taggart.

AUDITS AND ACCOUNTS, THE DIVISION OF; Tenth Floor, Municipal Building, Manhattan; Gordon T. Broad, *Auditor.*

BRADFORD STREET HOSPITAL, THE; 113 Bradford Street, Brooklyn; John F. FitzGerald, M.D., *General Medical Superintendent;* Margaret Lacey, *Chief Nurse.*

CENTRAL AND NEUROLOGICAL HOSPITAL, THE; Blackwell's Island, Manhattan; Charles B. Bacon, M.D., *Medical Superintendent.*

CHILDREN'S CLEARING BUREAU, THE; West Tremont and Andrews Avenues, Bronx; Ella A. Laurence, *Superintendent.*

CHILDREN'S HOME BUREAU, THE; 327 Schermerhorn Street, Brooklyn; John Daniels, *Director.*

CHILDREN'S HOSPITAL AND SCHOOL, THE NEW YORK CITY; Randall's Island, Manhattan; W. Burgess Cornell, M.D., *Medical Director.*

CITY HOSPITAL, THE NEW YORK; Blackwell's Island, Manhattan; Charles B. Bacon, M.D., *Medical Superintendent.*

CITY HOSPITAL SCHOOL OF NURSING, THE; Blackwell's Island, Manhattan; Carolyn E. Gray, *Superintendent.*

CONEY ISLAND HOSPITAL, THE; Ocean Parkway and Avenue Z, Brooklyn; Helene D. Bengston, *Acting Superintendent.*

CUMBERLAND STREET HOSPITAL, THE; 109 Cumberland Street, Brooklyn; Foster H. Platt, M.D., *Acting Superintendent.*

Cumberland Street Hospital Training School for Nurses, The; 109 Cumberland Street, Brooklyn; Imogene Miles, *Acting Superintendent.*

Drug Department, The General; Foot of East 26th Street, Manhattan; Frederick J. Kenney, *Chemist.*

Engineering Division, The; Tenth Floor, Municipal Building, Manhattan; John J. Herrick, *Chief Engineer.*

Food Bureau, The; Tenth Floor, Municipal Building, Manhattan; Louis J. McNally, *Departmental Steward.*

Greenpoint Hospital, The; Kingsland Avenue and Jackson Street, Brooklyn; John E. Daugherty, M.D., *Superintendent.*

Institutional Inspections, The Bureau of; 327 Schermerhorn Street, Brooklyn; Roy D. Bailey, *Director.*

Kings County Hospital, The; Clarkson Street near Albany Avenue, Brooklyn; John F. FitzGerald, M.D., *General Medical Superintendent;* Mortimer D. Jones, M.D., *Superintendent.*

Kings County Hospital Training School for Nurses, The; Clarkson Street near Albany Avenue, Brooklyn; Isabelle Burrows, *Superintendent.*

Laundries, The Departmental; Blackwell's Island, Manhattan; William J. Baade, *Superintendent.*

Mental Clinic, The; 57 East 125th Street, Manhattan, and 109 Cumberland Street, Brooklyn; W. Burgess Cornell, M.D., *Medical Director;* Nora McCarthy, *Nurse-in-Charge.*

Metropolitan Hospital, The; Blackwell's Island, Manhattan; Walter H. Conley, M.D., *Medical Superintendent.*

Metropolitan Hospital Training School for Nurses, The; Blackwell's Island, Manhattan; Agnes S. Ward, *Superintendent.*

Mortuary, The; First Avenue and 29th Street, Manhattan; Earl H. Burritt, *Superintendent.*

Municipal Lodging House, The; 432-8 East 25th Street, Manhattan; Stuart A. Rice, *Superintendent.*

Pass Bureau, The; Foot of East 70th Street, Manhattan; John D. Dolan, M.D., *Physician-in-Charge.*

Pathological Laboratories, The Manhattan; Blackwell's Island, Manhattan; John H. Larkin, M.D., *Pathologist.*

Pathological Laboratories, The Brooklyn; Clarkson Street near Albany Avenue, Brooklyn; Benjamin T. Terry, M.D., *Director.*

Pelham Bay Home, The; Hunter's Island, New York; Martha C. Gordon, *Supervising Nurse.*

Reception Hospital, The; Foot of East 70th Street, Manhattan; Walter H. Conley, M.D., *Medical Superintendent;* John D. Dolan, M.D., *Physician-in-Charge.*

Sea View Farms, The; (established in 1917 by the consolidation of The Sea View Hospital and The New York City Farm Colony) Castleton Corners, Richmond; William B. Buck, *Director.*

Secretary to the Commissioner; Tenth Floor, Municipal Building, Manhattan; Anna L. Lohman.

Secretary to the First Deputy Commissioner; Tenth Floor, Municipal Building, Manhattan; Lyman B. Stowe.

Secretary to the Second Deputy Commissioner; 327 Schermerhorn Street, Brooklyn; F. E. Brooke.

SECRETARY TO THE THIRD DEPUTY COMMISSIONER; Tenth Floor, Municipal Building, Manhattan; Thomas F. O'Mahoney.

SOCIAL INVESTIGATIONS, THE BUREAU OF; Tenth Floor, Municipal Building, Manhattan; Alexander M. Wilson, *Director;* Elizabeth M. Dinwiddie, *Assistant Director.*

DISTRICT OFFICES:

BRONX DISTRICT, THE; Arthur and Tremont Avenues, Bronx; Margaret Greene, *District Superintendent.*

GRAMERCY DISTRICT, THE; 289 Fourth Avenue, Manhattan; Florence B. Irvine, *District Superintendent.*

LOWER MANHATTAN DISTRICT, THE; Pearl and Centre Streets, Manhattan; Matilda M. Reamer, *District Superintendent.*

QUEENS DISTRICT, THE; Town Hall, Flushing, Queens; Eudora I. Davies, *District Superintendent.*

RICHMOND DISTRICT, THE; Borough Hall, St. George, Richmond; Eileen McGowan, *District Superintendent.*

SCHERMERHORN DISTRICT, THE; 327 Schermerhorn Street, Brooklyn; Anna C. Phillips, *District Superintendent.*

WILLIAMSBURGH DISTRICT, THE; 1022 Gates Avenue, Brooklyn; Mary J. Hickey, *District Superintendent.*

YORKVILLE DISTRICT, THE; 124 East 59th Street, Manhattan; Catherine M. Eagan, *District Superintendent.*

DOMESTIC RELATIONS, THE DIVISION OF:

Office for the Boroughs of Manhattan, Bronx and Richmond, 124 East 59th Street, Manhattan; Ida T. Upshaw, *Superintendent.* (The Alimony Division; Thomas F. Goaly, *Cashier.*)

Office for the Boroughs of Brooklyn and Queens, 383 Myrtle Avenue, Brooklyn; Ida May Robins, *Superintendent.* (The Alimony Division; Daniel J. O'Neill, *Cashier.*)

HOSPITAL DIVISION, THE:

Tenth Floor, Municipal Building, Manhattan; P. Joseph York, M.D., *Physician-in-Charge;* William H. Heaton, *Field Superintendent.*

SOCIAL SERVICE SECRETARIES:

Aged and Infirm, The New York City Home for the; SARAH JANE MANAHAN.

Central and Neurological Hospital, The; SARAH JANE MANAHAN.

Children's Hospital and School, The New York City; HELEN HEINRICHS.

City Hospital, The New York; MARY R. FLEMING.

Cumberland Street Hospital, The; LUCY A. CONNELLY.

Kings County Hospital, The; CAMILLE HARKINS.

Metropolitan Hospital, The; JESSIE C. PALMER.

Municipal Lodging House, The; JOSEPH B. ALDERMAN.

Sea View Farms, The; LILLIAN FEARN.

SOCIAL STATISTICS, THE BUREAU OF; Pearl and Centre Streets, Manhattan; I. M. Rubinow, Ph. D., *Director.*

STEAMBOATS, THE DEPARTMENTAL; Foot of East 26th Street, Manhattan; John J. Herrick, *Chief Engineer;* James E. Johnston, *Supervising Captain.*

STOREHOUSE, THE GENERAL; Blackwell's Island, Manhattan; Henry F. Scheitlin, *General Storekeeper.*

TUBERCULOSIS HOSPITAL ADMISSION BUREAU, THE; 426 First Avenue, Manhattan; G. Kremer, M.D., *Physician-in-Charge.*

Personnel

Baade, William J., *Superintendent,* The Departmental Laundries, Blackwell's Island, Manhattan.

Bacon, Charles B., M.D., *Medical Superintendent,* The New York City Hospital; The Central and Neurological Hospital; Blackwell's Island, Manhattan.

Bailey, Roy D., *Director,* The Bureau of Institutional Inspections, 327 Schermerhorn Street, Brooklyn.

Bengston, Helene D., *Acting Superintendent,* The Coney Island Hospital, Ocean Parkway and Avenue Z, Brooklyn.

Broad, Gordon T., *Auditor,* The Division of Audits and Accounts, Tenth Floor, Municipal Building, Manhattan.

Brooke, Frank E., *Secretary to the Second Deputy Commissioner,* 327 Schermerhorn Street, Brooklyn.

Buck, William B., *Director,* The Sea View Farms, Castleton Corners, Richmond.

Burritt, Earl H., *Superintendent,* The Mortuary, First Avenue and 29th Street, Manhattan.

Burrows, Isabelle, *Superintendent,* The Kings County Hospital Training School for Nurses, Clarkson Street near Albany Avenue, Brooklyn.

Conley, Walter H., M.D., *Medical Superintendent,* The Metropolitan Hospital, Blackwell's Island, Manhattan; Reception Hospital, Foot of East 70th Street, Manhattan.

Cornell, W. Burgess, M.D., *Medical Director,* The New York City Children's Hospital and School, Randall's Island, Manhattan; Mental Clinic, 57 East 125th Street, Manhattan, and 109 Cumberland Street, Brooklyn.

Daniels, John, *Director,* The Children's Home Bureau, 327 Schermerhorn Street, Brooklyn.

Daugherty, John E., M.D., *Superintendent,* The Greenpoint Hospital, Kingsland Avenue and Jackson Street, Brooklyn.

Davies, Eudora I., *District Superintendent,* Queens District Office, The Bureau of Social Investigations, Town Hall, Flushing, New York.

Dinwiddie, Elizabeth M., *Assistant Director,* The Bureau of Social Investigations, Tenth Floor, Municipal Building, Manhattan.

Dodworth, Victor S., *Secretary,* Department of Public Charities, Tenth Floor, Municipal Building, Manhattan.

Doherty, William J., *Second Deputy Commissioner,* 327 Schermerhorn Street, Brooklyn.

Dolan, John D., M.D., *Physician-in-Charge,* The Pass Bureau; The Reception Hospital, Foot of East 70th Street, Manhattan.

Eagan, Catherine M., *District Superintendent,* Yorkville District Office, The Bureau of Social Investigations, 124 East 59th Street, Manhattan.

Fernald, Walter E., M.D., *Expert Adviser,* The New York City Children's Hospital and School, Randall's Island, Manhattan. Residence: Massachusetts School for the Feeble-minded, Waverly, Mass.

Fiske, Floyd W., *Third Deputy Commissioner,* Tenth Floor, Municipal Building, Manhattan.

FitzGerald, John F., M.D., *General Medical Superintendent,* The Kings County Hospital; The Home for the Aged and Infirm (Brooklyn Division); Clarkson Street near Albany Avenue, Brooklyn; The Bradford Street Hospital, 113 Bradford Street, Brooklyn.

Gordon, Clifford J., *Assistant Secretary,* Tenth Floor, Municipal Building, Manhattan.

Gordon, Martha C., *Supervising Nurse,* The Pelham Bay Home, Hunters Island, New York.

Gray, Carolyn E., *Superintendent,* The City Hospital School of Nursing, Blackwell's Island, Manhattan.

Greene, Margaret, *District Superintendent,* Bronx District Office, The Bureau of Social Investigations, Bergen Building, Arthur and Tremont Avenues, Bronx.

Heaton, William H., *Field Supervisor,* Hospital Division, The Bureau of Social Investigations, Tenth Floor, Municipal Building, Manhattan.

Herrick, John J., *Chief Engineer,* The Engineering Division, Tenth Floor, Municipal Building, Manhattan.

Hickey, Mary J., *District Superintendent,* Williamsburgh District Office, The Bureau of Social Investigations, 1022 Gates Avenue, Brooklyn.

Irvine, Florence B., *District Superintendent,* Gramercy District Office, The Bureau of Social Investigations, 289 Fourth Avenue, Manhattan.

Johnston, James E., *Supervising Captain,* The Departmental Steamboats, Foot of East 26th Street, Manhattan.

Jones, Mortimer D., M.D., *Superintendent,* The Kings County Hospital, Clarkson Street near Albany Avenue, Brooklyn.

Kenney, Frederick J., *Chemist,* The General Drug Department, Foot of East 26th Street, Manhattan.

Kingsbury, John A., *Commissioner,* Tenth Floor, Municipal Building, Manhattan.

Kremer, G., M.D., *Physician-in-Charge,* The Tuberculosis Hospital Admission Bureau, 426 First Avenue, Manhattan.

Lamb, Bernard, *Contract Clerk,* Tenth Floor, Municipal Building, Manhattan.

Lacey, Margaret, *Chief Nurse,* The Bradford Street Hospital, 118 Bradford Street, Brooklyn.

Larkin, John H., M.D., *Pathologist,* The Manhattan Pathological Laboratories, Blackwell's Island, Manhattan.

Laurence, Ella A., *Superintendent,* The Children's Clearing Bureau, West Tremont and Andrews Avenues, Bronx.

Lohmann, Anna L., *Secretary to the Commissioner,* Tenth Floor, Municipal Building, Manhattan.

McCarthy, Nora, *Nurse-in-Charge,* Mental Clinic, 57 East 125th Street, Manhattan, and 109 Cumberland Street, Brooklyn.

McGowan, Eileen, *District Superintendent,* Richmond District Office, The Bureau of Social Investigations, Borough Hall, St. George, Richmond.

McMahon, Edward E., *Superintendent,* The New York City Home for the Aged and Infirm, Blackwell's Island, Manhattan.

McNally, Louis J., *Departmental Steward,* The Food Bureau, Tenth Floor, Municipal Building, Manhattan.

O'Mahoney, Thomas J., *Secretary to the Third Deputy Commissioner,* Tenth Floor, Municipal Building, Manhattan.

Phillips, Anna C., *District Superintendent,* Schermerhorn District Office, The Bureau of Social Investigations, 327 Schermerhorn Street, Brooklyn.

Price, Thomas I., M.D., *Deputy Medical Superintendent,* The Home for the Aged and Infirm (Brooklyn Division), Clarkson Street near Albany Avenue, Brooklyn.

Reamer, Matilda M., *District Superintendent,* Lower Manhattan District Office, The Bureau of Social Investigations, Centre and Pearl Streets, Manhattan.

Rice, Stuart A., *Superintendent,* The Municipal Lodging House, 432 East 25th Street, Manhattan.

Robins, Ida May, *Superintendent,* The Division of Domestic Relations; The Bureau of Social Investigations, 383 Myrtle Avenue, Brooklyn.

Rubinow, I. M., Ph.D., *Director,* The Bureau of Social Statistics, Pearl and Centre Streets, Manhattan.

Scheitlin, Henry F., *General Storekeeper,* The General Storehouse, Blackwell's Island, Manhattan.

Stowe, Lyman B., *Secretary to the First Deputy Commissioner,* Tenth Floor, Municipal Building, Manhattan.

Terry, Benjamin T., M.D., *Director,* The Brooklyn Pathological Laboratories, Clarkson Street near Albany Avenue, Brooklyn.

Upshaw, Ida T., *Superintendent,* The Division of Domestic Relations, The Bureau of Social Investigations, 124 East 59th Street, Manhattan.

Ward, Agnes S., *Superintendent,* The Metropolitan Hospital Training School for Nurses, Blackwell's Island, Manhattan.

Wilson, Alexander M., *Director,* The Bureau of Social Investigations, Tenth Floor, Municipal Building, Manhattan.

Wright, Henry C., *First Deputy Commissioner,* Tenth Floor, Municipal Building, Manhattan.

York, P. Joseph, M.D., *Physician-in-Charge,* The Hospital Division, The Bureau of Social Investigations, Tenth Floor, Municipal Building, Manhattan.

Advisory Committees

Children's Hospital and School, The New York City; Charles L. Dana, M.D., *Chairman,* 53 West 53rd Street, Manhattan; Eleanor Hope Johnson, *Secretary,* 77 Irving Place, Manhattan; Walter E. Fernald, M.D., *Expert Adviser,* Massachusetts School for the Feeble-minded, Waverly, Mass.

City Hospital, The New York; Mrs. M. Cadwalader Jones, Chairman, 21 East 11th Street, Manhattan; Mary R. Fleming, *Secretary,* The New York City Hospital, Blackwell's Island, Manhattan.

Cumberland Street Hospital, The; Herbert C. Allen, M.D., *Chairman,* 171 Lefferts Place, Brooklyn; Mrs. J. Hubley Schall, *Secretary,* 119 St. Mark's Avenue, Brooklyn.

Kings County Hospital, The; Mrs. F. L. Cranford, *Chairman,* 479 Clinton Avenue, Brooklyn; Daisy Gans, *Secretary,* 497 Halsey Street, Brooklyn.

Metropolitan Hospital, The; Mrs. William K. Draper, *Chairman,* 121 East 36th Street, Manhattan; Bailey B. Burritt, *Secretary,* 105 East 22nd Street, Manhattan.

Municipal Lodging House, The; John B. Andrews, *Chairman,* 131 East 23rd Street, Manhattan; Stuart A. Rice, *Secretary,* 432-8 East 25th Street, Manhattan.

Sea View Farms, The; Mrs. Rogers H. Bacon, *Chairman,* 987 Madison Avenue, Manhattan; Mrs. Yale Kneeland, *Secretary,* 117 East 60th Street, Manhattan.

Medical Boards

Central and Neurological Hospital, The; Ernest F. Krug, M.D., *President,* 12 West 44th Street, Manhattan; Henry House Beers, M.D., *Secretary,* 40 West 41st Street, Manhattan.

Children's Hospital and School, The New York City; Samuel Dana Hubbard, M.D., *Chairman,* 143 West 103rd Street, Manhattan; Edward Wright Peet, M.D., *Secretary,* 144 West 93rd Street, Manhattan.

City Hospital, The New York; Daniel S. Dougherty, M.D., *President,* 156 West 73rd Street, Manhattan; Orrin Sage Wightman, M.D., *Secretary,* 113 West 78th Street, Manhattan.

Coney Island Hospital, The; Joseph P. Murphy, M.D., *President,* 653 St. Mark's Avenue, Brooklyn; Judson P. Pendleton, M.D., *Secretary,* 95 Sixth Avenue, Brooklyn.

Cumberland Street Hospital, The; Charles L. Johnston, M.D., *Chairman,* 232 Hancock Street, Brooklyn; John F. Rankin, M.D., *Secretary,* 852 Park Place, Brooklyn.

Greenpoint Hospital, The; H. Beekman Delatour, M.D., 73 Eighth Avenue, Brooklyn; Robert L. Dickinson, M.D., *Secretary,* 168 Clinton Street, Brooklyn.

Kings County Hospital, The; Calvin Premyre Barber, M.D., *President,* 57 South Oxford Street, Brooklyn; Leo J. J. Commiskey, M.D., *Secretary,* 189 Sixth Avenue, Brooklyn.

Metropolitan Hospital, The; E. G. Rankin, M.D., *Superintendent,* 175 West 58th Street, Manhattan; G. S. Harrington, M.D., *Secretary,* 187 West 145th Street, Manhattan.

Sea View Farms, The; Frederick Coonley, M.D., President, 83 Livingston Place, West New Brighton, Richmond; Charles Lawrence Allers, M.D., *Secretary,* 34 Fort Place, New Brighton, Richmond.

Clinics

Cardiac:

The Cumberland Street Hospital; Thursdays, 7 P.M.—9 P.M.

Children's:

The Cumberland Street Hospital; Mondays, Wednesdays and Fridays, 10 A.M.—12 M.

The Greenpoint Hospital; Mondays, Wednesdays and Fridays, 1 P.M.—3 P.M.

The Kings County Hospital; Tuesdays, Thursdays and Saturdays, 1 P.M. —2 P.M.

Dental:

The Cumberland Street Hospital; Tuesdays and Fridays, 2 P.M.—4 P.M.

Ear:

The Kings County Hospital; Fridays, 2 P.M.—3 P.M.

Eye:

The Greenpoint Hospital; Mondays, Wednesdays and Fridays, 1 P.M.—3 P.M.

Eye and Ear:

The Cumberland Street Hospital; Tuesdays and Fridays, 2 P.M.—4 P.M.

General Clinic:

The Kings County Hospital; every day except Sunday, 9 A.M.—12 M.

Genito-Urinary:

The Greenpoint Hospital; Mondays, Wednesdays and Fridays, 11 A.M.—12 M.

Gynecological:

The Cumberland Street Hospital; Tuesdays and Fridays, 2 P.M.—4 P.M.
The Coney Island Hospital; every day except Sunday, 10 A.M.—12 A.M.
The Greenpoint Hospital; Mondays, Wednesdays and Fridays, 1 P.M.—12 A.M.
The Kings County Hospital; Mondays and Fridays, 2 P.M.—4 P.M.

Massage:

The Kings County Hospital; Mondays, Wednesdays and Fridays, 10 A.M.

Medical:

The Coney Island Hospital; every day except Sunday, 10 A.M.—12 M.
The Greenpoint Hospital; Mondays, Wednesdays and Fridays, 1 P.M.—3 P.M.

Mental:

The Cumberland Street Hospital; Mondays and Tuesdays, 9 A.M.—12 M.
57 East 125th Street, Manhattan; Wednesdays, Thursdays, Fridays and Saturdays, 9 A.M.—12 M.

Nervous:

The Kings County Hospital; Wednesdays and Saturdays, 2 P.M.—4 P.M.

Nose and Throat:

The Cumberland Street Hospital; Thursdays, 10 A.M.—12 M.
The Greenpoint Hospital; Mondays, Wednesdays and Fridays, 2 P.M.—3 P.M.
The Kings County Hospital; Mondays, 2 P.M.—4 P.M., and Thursdays, 2 P.M.—3 P.M.

Obstetrical:

The Greenpoint Hospital; Mondays, Wednesdays and Fridays, 11 A.M.—12 M.
The Kings County Hospital; Tuesdays and Thursdays, 2 P.M.—4 P.M.

Poliomyelitis:

The Greenpoint Hospital; every day except Sunday, 9 A.M.—1 P.M.
112 Broadway, Flushing, Queens; Mondays, Wednesdays and Fridays, 10 A.M.—12 M.
138 Hunter Avenue, Long Island City, Queens; Mondays and Fridays, 3 P.M.—5 P.M.

Prenatal:

The Cumberland Street Hospital; Wednesdays, 2 P.M.—4 P.M.

Skin:

The Greenpoint Hospital; Fridays, 3 P.M.—4 P.M.
The Kings County Hospital; Tuesdays, 2 P.M.—4 P.M.

Surgical:

The Coney Island Hospital; every day except Sunday, 10 A.M.—12 M.
The Greenpoint Hospital; Mondays, Wednesdays and Fridays, 9 A.M.—10 A.M.

www.ingramcontent.com/pod-product-compliance
Lightning Source LLC
LaVergne TN
LVHW010610110826
845149LV00003B/850

* 9 7 8 1 4 1 8 1 8 7 2 4 8 *